G000166995

I Want to Talk With
my TEEN About
GIRL STUFF

BY

HEATHER FLIES

Standard
P U B L I S H I N G
Bringing The Word to Life

Cincinnati, Ohio

Credits

I Want to Talk With My Teen About Girl Stuff
© 2006 Standard Publishing, Cincinnati, Ohio. A division of Standex International Corporation. All rights reserved. Printed in China.

All rights reserved. No part of this book may be reproduced in any manner whatsoever without written permission from the publisher, except where noted in the text and in the case of brief quotations embodied in critical articles and reviews.

Credits
Produced by Susan Lingo Books™
Cover by Diana Walters

All Scripture quotations, unless otherwise indicated, are taken from the HOLY BIBLE, NEW INTERNATIONAL VERSION®. NIV®. Copyright © 1973, 1978, 1984 by International Bible Society. Used by permission of Zondervan Publishing House. All rights reserved.

13 12 11 10 09 08 07 06   9 8 7 6 5 4 3 2 1
0-7847-1895-4

Contents

Introduction

What kinds of things are "girl stuff," and why should I talk with my daughter about them?

Braces. High-pitched laughs. Slumber parties. Makeup. Boys. Mood swings. So often, we identify things in the life of a teenage girl as surface, insignificant, or just plain silly. The truth is, despite the superficial appearance, each element symbolizes and reflects the intense emotions and changes taking place in the life of a young woman. When we take the time to notice, we not only validate the changes, but we also begin to understand who she is and who she desperately wants to become.

I Want to Talk With My Teen About Girl Stuff is your everyday guide to understanding the teenage girl in your life. It was written to offer information, encouragement, insight, and practical help for those who care about teen girls. As you turn the pages, you'll be reminded of the normalcy of a girl's struggle with self-esteem as well as the importance of God's part in conquering that struggle. We'll delve into the confusing world of relationships with family, friends, and boyfriends—acknowledging the needs and challenges within those relationships.

Teenage girls are longing for the adults in their lives to slow down and take notice of them. And this includes every girl: the one who dresses immodestly; the one who has bought into the lie of the "perfect" body; the one who doesn't feel as if she measures up to other girls; even the girl who seems to measure up. Let's be the ones who notice them—and *I Want to Talk With My Teen About Girl Stuff* is a great place to start!

Heather Flies

Where Do You Stand?

Walking alongside your daughter as she moves through adolescence is difficult, thrilling, and confusing—at the same time! The following questionnaire will help you evaluate your own strengths and weaknesses and where your own values and philosophies fit in. Circle the box with the number that best corresponds to your answer. Then add up the total of your answers and check out the How You Scored box! (Retake the quiz after reading the book to see if your score changed!)

OPTIONS

❶ Strongly agree

❷ Agree somewhat

❸ Disagree somewhat

❹ Strongly disagree

I REGULARLY ASK MY DAUGHTER TO INVITE HER FRIENDS TO OUR HOUSE FOR SOCIAL TIMES.

❶　❷　❸　❹

I'VE SHARED WITH MY DAUGHTER SOME OF MY SEXUAL BOUNDARIES AND STRUGGLES WHEN I WAS A TEEN.

❶　❷　❸　❹

I HANDLE CONFLICTS WITH FAMILY, FRIENDS, AND CO-WORKERS IN HEALTHY, GODLY WAYS.

❶　❷　❸　❹

I HAVE STRONG SELF-ESTEEM AND AM INTENTIONAL ABOUT STRENGTHENING IT.

❶　❷　❸　❹

I CHOOSE THE "PARENT HAT"
OVER THE "FRIEND HAT" WHEN
INTERACTING WITH MY TEEN.

❶ ❷ ❸ ❹

I TAKE CARE OF MY BODY AND
ENCOURAGE MY FAMILY MEMBERS
TO DO THE SAME.

❶ ❷ ❸ ❹

I REGULARLY INITIATE DISCUSSIONS
WITH MY TEEN ABOUT SEX, DATING,
OR RELATIONSHIPS.

❶ ❷ ❸ ❹

IN OUR FAMILY, CONSEQUENCES
ARE IMPLEMENTED WHEN
GUIDELINES ARE BROKEN.

❶ ❷ ❸ ❹

EVEN AS AN ADULT, I CONTINUE
TO HONOR AND RESPECT MY
PARENTS.

❶ ❷ ❸ ❹

I PLAY AN ACTIVE ROLE IN
THE FRIENDSHIP CHOICES MY
DAUGHTER MAKES.

❶ ❷ ❸ ❹

HOW YOU SCORED

10—20 Give yourself a pat on the back! You have an honest perspective on yourself and are intentional about helping your daughter do the same. You take your role as parent seriously and spend time investing in your daughter. As she watches you, she will have a tangible model of a godly person.

21—31 Your perspective on the issues your daughter faces may need a bit of focusing. You desire to be honest and open to discussing tough topics, but you may find yourself feeling uncertain in the world of today's young girls. Be encouraged knowing that as you invest in your own self-esteem, relationships, and conflict resolution, the result will be reflected in your relationship with your daughter as well.

32—40 Perhaps you're still struggling with where you fit in. You long to invest in your daughter so she can develop into a healthy, God-fearing, well-balanced young woman, but you may be overwhelmed. Start with small steps and pray for God's leading. Your daughter will thank you!

Growing in His Image

Throughout history, various forces have shaped young women. From biblical times when older women trained up godly women to today's beer ads, super-thin models, and reality TV shows with destructive messages, it's time to bring our girls back to the true source of their identities while empowering them to be all God created them to be.

God created us uniquely.

Society tells our girls that their worth is based on outward appearances. Their Creator reassures them that their worth comes from the fact that he created them and sent his Son to die for them. As adults, we need to help clear out society's mixed messages so our girls can hear the gentle whisper of the One who adores them.

Individuality is a gift from God.

Psalm 139 proclaims that we were knit together in our mother's wombs. As with most of King David's writings, he doesn't leave it at the facts—he moves to the descriptive and tells us that we are "fearfully and wonderfully made." As hard as I try, I can't imagine God deciding that each human being would be fearfully and wonderfully made in the exact same way. To do so would be in direct contradiction with his creative character. Instead of a cookie-cutter mentality, the great Creator fashioned everyone with individual traits, gifts, and quirks—and I am thankful he did!

key point
FOCUS ON CHARACTER, NOT JUST APPEARANCE.

key point
INSPIRE A HEALTHY SELF-PERSPECTIVE.

Unfortunately, our society has not adopted the same philosophy. If you ask a classroom of girls to draw pictures of the ideal teenage girl, you'd be amazed in the similarities woven through each drawing: skinny build, big chest, blonde hair, smart, confident, sexy, athletic, and fashionable. But what about the girl who has a small chest or is shy? How about the girl who plays football with the guys or is most comfortable in sweats and a T-shirt? According to much of society, there is no room for her—at least not in the groups that seem to matter.

DID YOU KNOW THAT one in three articles in teen girls magazines includes a focus on appearance, and 50% of their advertisers use an appeal to beauty to sell their products?

Yet the Lord created the shy girl and is delighted with her sweet spirit! God shaped the athletic girl's muscles to be strong and her movements smooth. Individuality is an incredible gift—yet many girls are tempted to throw these gifts aside in order to fit a mold that has been set for them by movies, music videos, and magazines. Many girls sense they are meant to be something more, but when they attempt to express or use their gifts, they are often shut down.

In order to help young women claim the God-given gift of individuality, we need to reevaluate what messages we're communicating to our girls about their inner qualities as well as outer appearances.

MIDDLE-SCHOOL MEMOS

One of the ways middle-school girls reflect their individuality is through creativity. Even if your daughter's art or music is a bit hard to understand, celebrate the uniqueness that God created within her!

Gender is a gift from God.

Genesis 1:27 tells us that *"God created man in his own image, in the image of God he created him; male and female he created them."* From the beginning, God has celebrated

key point
GOD CREATED BOTH MALES AND FEMALES.

gender. While day and night, birds, fish, and animals were "good," God looked at Adam and Eve, as male and female, and proclaimed them "very good." Remember that sin had not yet entered the world—everything was just as God intended it to be.

key point
BOTH GENDERS ARE EQUALLY IMPORTANT!

According to Genesis, the Lord took dust from the ground and formed Adam. He breathed the breath of life into his nostrils, and Adam became a living being. Incredible! No blueprints to be drawn up. No working prototypes to be tested. The God of the universe simply breathed life into Adam and began the human race. As the man of the garden, Adam was placed in charge of Eden and of all living creatures dwelling within its boundaries. He named the animals. He delivered baby calves. He probably even spoke kind words to the tomatoes as they grew. Yet something was missing.

STOP & CONSIDER

- How do I talk about the opposite gender?

- What do I value about my gender?

- How can I help my daughter embrace being a woman?

"When men and women are able to respect and accept their differences, then love has a chance to blossom." —John Gray

God said, *"It is not good for the man to be alone"* (Genesis 2:18). At this point, God could have solved the problem in many ways—another animal, a brother. Instead, God chose to create Eve. As Adam slept, God took part of him and made the companion Adam would spend his life loving. Eve was different. Adam's skin was tight and covered with coarse hair, while Eve's was soft and smooth. Adam approached the animals with power and demanded their attention; she walked slowly, touched softly, and spoke tenderly. And God said it was "very good."

When your daughter is frustrated with boys, help her see the good things guys bring to relationships, including levelheadedness, analysis, and strength.

TRY THESE!

Set magazine pictures of guys and girls side by side, then list their similarities and differences. Discuss why God chose to create each.

Ask your daughter what she would love about being a guy. Common answers are "getting ready in ten minutes" or "no periods."

Read aloud Psalm 139:13, 14 with your daughter. Remind her that God made her exactly as he desired her to be and that she can celebrate her gender in wondrous ways!

In a time when gender lines are often blurred, teenagers can miss the beauty of gender. Help your daughter identify and celebrate things that reflect her femininity. When she cries, remind her that God gave her a kind and compassionate heart. As she develops hips, talk to her about the blessing of being able to have babies. In the same way, highlight traits that reflect the masculinity of boys. Say things such as, "Isn't it great that God gave Kyle such an analytical mind!" or "I'm so thankful your father is a wonderful provider." The end result will be a woman who values her femininity and respects the masculinity of men.

Jesus is the ultimate role model.

So often in the Christian world, kids can feel overwhelmed by the expectations adults set for them. We mean well. We ask them to go to church, to be responsible in their studies, disciplined in their sports, pure in their sexual boundaries, committed to cleaning their rooms, wise with their money, kind to the elderly, respectful of authority, dedicated in the reading of their Bibles, and … you get the idea. All these expectations are valid and beneficial, but they are often driven by our own agendas and preferences rather than by the desired results.

> **key point**
> OUR GOAL IS TO BE MORE LIKE JESUS.

> **key point**
> JESUS STAYED FOCUSED ON HIS CALLING.

What if we challenged kids to be like Christ?

Throughout Scripture, we are called to be holy, as when 1 Peter 1:15 reminds us to: *"Be holy in all you do."* As ones created in the image of God, what better model can we find than Jesus himself? The Gospels are filled with examples of Jesus' compassion, direct communication, patience, and genuine concern for people. As we study those examples, we can find ways to make Jesus' holiness real in our own lives. Jesus wasn't weak. He didn't let people get away with things. He stayed focused on his calling. Jesus is the ultimate role model!

BIG BIBLE POINT

Share Mark 1:40, 41 with your daughter. Discuss how we can touch "untouchables" and have compassion for those in need.

Encourage your daughter to express concern for others.

MIDDLE-SCHOOL MEMOS

Share a time when you made the choice to be Christ-like. Be specific. Be authentic. What was difficult about the situation? What was rewarding about your choice?

A teenage girl has a wide variety of role models to choose from. If her goal is to sing, act, and marry a cute guy, she can strive to be like Jessica Simpson. If she'd rather pose seductively on the cover of *Entertainment Weekly* by age 18, Lindsay Lohan is the one whose footsteps she'll want to follow. Of course, there's no guarantee either of these girls will be around long enough for anyone to follow. Jesus said, *"I am the vine; you are the branches. If a man remains in me and I in him, he will bear much fruit; apart from me you can do nothing"* (John 15:5). Now, that's a guarantee!

TRY THIS!

Each day, read a passage from the Gospels highlighting Jesus' interaction with a person or group. Ask, "What would be your response in this situation?"

If a young girl takes the challenge and holds tightly to the vine, she "will bear much fruit." That fruit, listed in Galatians 5:22, 23, includes love, joy, peace, patience, kindness, goodness, faithfulness, gentleness, and self-control. As she daily remains in Jesus, she will find herself loving the unlovable. Others will marvel at her peace amidst the storms of life. Joy will flow from her heart even in the midst of trial. Her words and touch will communicate gentleness to those around her. She will be faithful in her relationships. She will be like Christ.

Do I seek holiness in my own life?

Do I challenge my daughter to be more like Christ?

What fruit of the Spirit do I see in my daughter?

Does our family often ask: "How would Jesus respond?"

It's not bad, just different.

Teen girls are just discovering that guys and girls are different. Thanks to media and movies centered on aggressive, heroic women, girls may begin to think that females have it all and that guys are lacking. A healthy way to look at the many differences in guys and girls is this: *It's not bad, just different.*

Girls think differently than guys.

I am intrigued by conversations I hear as I drive the bus for our junior-high events. From the boys comes a constant flow of statistics and information. They talk in excited tones about the NFL standings and how they affect their fantasy football teams. The discussions may be briefly interrupted as a sports car drives near the bus. "Check out that Dodge Viper with the V-12!" A few rows back, the girls huddle to discuss the latest breakup between Travis and Lindsey. "I can't believe he did it through a note," and "I totally know he likes Kelly!"

key point
WE LISTEN AND SPEAK DIFFERENTLY.

key point
WE THINK AND REACT DIFFERENTLY.

Both males and females are influenced by what they value. Girls value relationships and emotions. Guys value information and activity. Just observe a group of teens at a Super Bowl party. Girls bounce around the room excited by being with friends. They position themselves strategically around the guys. Guys think of the girls when they walk in front of the TV or when they're bearing gifts of food. Other than that, they're simply there to watch the game.

Girls process feelings and information through talking. If they're in emotional turmoil, relief comes from talking through the situation—over and over with friends. As they talk and receive responses, they begin to gain understanding of the situation. Guys deal with their thoughts more internally and may withdraw from relational contact to reflect and process. Well-meaning girls may attempt to tap into a guy's thoughts before the reflection has taken place, but they will be unsuccessful.

Dads, listen for underlying messages in your daughter's fast-paced talking. Is she nervous, excited, or afraid? You may not decipher every thought and emotion, but listening is a great place to start!

GUYS ...
- **Value information and activity.**
- **Process through private reflection.**

Guys and Girls Think & React Differently!

GIRLS ...
- **Value relationships and emotions.**
- **Process through talking with others.**

To be helpful to the girls in our lives, we need to acknowledge the emotions and intensity that go hand in hand with a girl's thinking. If you desire to hear her thoughts, you first must validate her intense feelings. Ask her what she is feeling and really take the time to listen. Offer responses such as, "I can see why you would be so sad," or "That must be so frustrating." Once she is able to deal with the emotions in a safe way, she'll be more likely to process her thoughts with you.

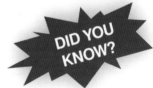

DID YOU KNOW?

Scientists have studied the processing abilities of guys and found it can take up to seven hours to return to and process an emotion they felt earlier. As frustrating as this can be for girls, it gives guys the ability to be more objective.

Girls relate differently than guys.

Picture an outdoor sports complex with a baseball diamond on the left and a softball diamond on the right. On the right, you see the ponytails of the girls bouncing up and down as they excitedly recite the cheer they created on the bus ride to the field. Glance to the left and you see a bench filled with boys chewing sunflower seeds, kicking dirt off their cleats, mentally preparing for their turns at bat, and pretty much ignoring each other—with the exception of an occasional high five or pat on the butt. They're engaging in the same type of event, but they obviously have a different way of relating with each other.

key point
WE ALL RELATE IN UNIQUE WAYS.

key point
EXPERIENCES AFFECT HOW WE RELATE.

When we boil it down, girls relate through talking, sharing, and anything else in the verbal realm. Guys relate through activity. The boys on the baseball bench are not having an inadequate experience when compared to the girls. Just the opposite—they're completely content to stay in their personal zones and experience the game.

✓ **MIDDLE-SCHOOL MEMOS**
When you are spending time with middle-school girls, *what* you are doing really isn't the most important thing. The value lies in time spent and thoughts shared.

"I love talking to you because you don't freak out or judge me. You just listen. You understand."
—Audrey, 14

For guys, unlike girls, success in sports has nothing to do with feeling good about one another. It's about competition and being physical. Sure, girls enjoy the game, but what they enjoy even more is talking on the bus ride home—talking about the game, the cheers, and the cute boys who came to watch. The guys' bus? Probably quiet.

> Hormone levels determine actions. Testosterone drives guys' interest in football, guns, and more. Women may enjoy these activities too, but aren't preoccupied with them (from *Bringing Up Boys*, James C. Dobson, 2001).

- Do I do more talking or listening with my daughter?

- What can I affirm in my daughter's thought process that is different from my own?

- How can I validate my daughter's feelings on a daily basis?

- How can I help my daughter relate to others in healthy ways?

Of course, there are exceptions. Some girls love the thrill of competition and quickly get annoyed when their girlfriends *talk* more than *compete*. Some guys like a lot of chatter on the bench and don't understand when their teammates get riled up about a call. However, these are definitely exceptions to the norm. Girls, who relate by spending time together and talking, are drawn to coffee shops, talking on the phone, writing cards, or sitting on the deck. The average guy relates to softball tournaments, golf, NASCAR, and video games. Each gives both guys and girls opportunities to relate with others while being involved in activities with a purpose.

REMEMBER:
It's not bad, just different.

Both genders are equal in God's eyes.

key point
BOTH GENDERS ARE LOVED BY GOD.

Perhaps you've heard someone say, "God didn't get it right with Adam, but he perfected it with Eve." We laugh it off as Christian humor, but an underlying message looms beneath the surface: men and women are not equal in God's eyes. Nothing could be further from the truth!

key point
CHRIST DIED FOR US ALL.

The Lord loves all of his children no matter the gender, skin color, economic status, or sin record. In Genesis, God created male and female in his image and claimed they were "very good." Although different, each is valued and loved equally by God.

Chooses us

Saves us

GOD GIVES US ALL EQUAL BILLING! HE ...

Uses us

Loves us

If the creation account doesn't convince you that God views both genders the same, simply start turning the pages of the Bible. According to his sovereign will, God used both men and women in powerful ways to accomplish his will. For the freeing of the Israelites, God called Moses. When the Jews were about to be eliminated as a group, the Lord raised up young Esther to step in and intervene. Through God's power and purpose, Moses, Esther, and hundreds of other men and women were used by God—and loved by him.

God doesn't play favorites — he loves us all!

BIG BIBLE POINT

Because of Jesus' death and resurrection, we all have equal status. Read Galatians 3:28, 29 and discuss the following:

- What comparisons could we add to Paul's list?
- How is this freedom lived out in our lives?
- What does it mean to be "heirs" of Jesus Christ?

Paul, as the author of the letters to Corinth, goes into detail about spiritual gifts in 1 Corinthians 12:4-6: *"There are different kinds of gifts, but the same Spirit. There are different kinds of service, but the same Lord. There are different kinds of working, but the same God works all of them in all men."* Paul does not write about different genders, only about different parts of the body of Christ. To compare the eye or hand to another part of the body and conclude it's not valued would be irrational. Similarly, God needs *both* men and women to carry out the purpose for his body of believers and for the world.

God has great plans in store for your daughter! Remind your daughter that God knows the plans he has laid out for her (Jeremiah 29:11) and is working that plan out with love every day. Remind her that God delights in who she was created to be. What incredible truths! The cool thing is, God feels the same way about guys—celebrating and using the uniquenesses in them to complete his will. And as the ultimate sign of equal love and value, God sent his Son to die on the cross for *all* of us!

Girls need to know that God has special plans for their lives.

Brainstorm how God chose different women in the Bible to accomplish his will. Chat about why God may have used them for those tasks and how God has a plan for each girl's life today.

Know what a godly woman is like.

Most young girls are aware of rules and expectations: Don't have sex before you're married. Love everyone. Choose good friends. Be respectful. If we desire our girls to be godly women, we need to be certain they know what a godly woman looks like.

Godly women are strong on the inside.

The average teenager wakes up to her CD alarm clock, walks through a day full of distractions, and falls asleep with her iPod playing. Not much time for personal reflection or solitude. In order for a young woman to be strong on the inside, she needs to know herself—and that can happen only when she takes time to look deeper than the curl in her hair or the shape of her body. But looking deep is scary. A godly woman claims victory over that fear. She takes time to allow God to search her heart and teach her about herself.

key point

INTERNAL PURPOSE EQUALS OUTWARD CONFIDENCE.

Being STRONG on the outside requires STRENGTH from the inside!

As a godly woman discovers who she is, she is able to discern her purpose and understand what God intends for her life. She realizes her love for people with disabilities as she visits with special-ed students in the school lunch room. She senses the Lord's pleasure as she leads worship in youth group. Whatever it may be, her internal sense of purpose will give her visible confidence.

CHAPTER 1 — GROWING IN HIS IMAGE

Read Lamentations 3:22, 23, then ask yourself:

- What emotion most easily consumes my daughter?
- Why should we not be consumed, according to these verses?
- How has God shown his faithfulness to us in the past?
- What would an emotionally balanced teenage girl be like?

No one likes to be critiqued. When feedback comes our way, we often become defensive and lash back at the one attempting to address an area of growth. As a girl is molded and shaped to be more like her Creator, she must be able to accept a loving, constructive act of criticism. Why? Because she knows that some pruning must happen in order for her to be a reflection of God's character. Instead of taking every critique personally, she sees it as an opportunity to grow. And rather than pointing a finger back at the messenger, she must assess whether the critique is true and what she can do to prune that particular area of her life.

MIDDLE-SCHOOL MEMOS

Middle schoolers often send messages that say, "We want noise and distraction all the time!" Although most enjoy the chaos, they long for quiet time—they just don't know it. Structure quiet time for your middle schooler, and she will begin to long for it.

TARGET MOMENT

The next time your daughter is critiqued by someone, process it through with her. Set your defensiveness aside to help her find opportunities for pruning within the tough-to-hear feedback.

The teenage years, especially for girls, are flooded with emotions. A godly girl is one who has found that time and intensity are the keys to being emotionally balanced. Feeling fear or loneliness is natural, but allowing these emotions to lead to poor choices is not healthy. Godly girls feel emotions but do not allow themselves to be consumed by them.

Godly women are secure on the outside.

As I walk down the halls of our junior and senior high schools, I am intrigued by the different types of girls and how they carry themselves. *Type one* walks down the side of the hallway, eyes to the floor, hoping to blend in and not be noticed. *Type two* walks with her chest out, pants low or skirt high, and face eager. She desperately wants to be noticed by the guys. *Type three* walks confidently down the center of the hallway, greeting others with eye contact and a kind smile. She is dressed cute but modestly.

A godly girl should naturally be a *type-three* girl. Her inner security, sense of purpose, and emotional balance allow her to look people in the eyes and walk through the day with confidence. But it doesn't stop there! Godly girls initiate conversations and relationships with people. The teachers are not seen as enemies but as partners in learning. The new kid at school is not seen as an outsider but as a potential friend. According to John 15:5, when we are connected to the Lord, we will "bear much fruit." Godly girls are connected to others because they're connected to Christ.

KINDNESS

JOY

GENTLENESS

LOVE

COMPASSION

Godly girls bear good fruit!

The really cool part about godly girls being secure on the inside and the outside is that they become magnetic! In the midst of peers who are striving simply to survive the day, *type-three* girls are seen as a wonder. Others see a secure girl and think, "What's she have that I don't?" or "I want to be like her." Some observe from afar; others try to get close to see if she's for real. At those moments, she has the opportunity to touch the lives of others—and she wants to! From her humble position, she can encourage, comfort, and even inspire her peers.

key point
GODLY GIRLS ARE CONNECTED TO GOD.

key point
GODLY GIRLS TOUCH PEOPLE'S LIVES.

TAKE 5

* Are you willing to take risks in your own life?
* Do you encourage your daughter to take risks?
* Do you model a godly woman or just communicate general guidelines?
* Do you take time for personal reflection and growth?
* How can you help your daughter become more secure about herself?

When God is at the center of a girl's life, freedom reigns! She is able to try new things because she's assured that her worth isn't based on performance. When fear and anxiety might normally prevail, a godly girl steps out of her comfort zone, takes risks, and says, "I'll try it!" Not making a team or being made fun of because she is in the chess club doesn't faze her because value comes in a solid relationship with Christ and his design for her life. Freedom!

STOP & CONSIDER

Your daughter learns from watching you. Be intentional about trying something you're not guaranteed to succeed at—such as snowboarding, singing karaoke, or even teaching Sunday school—and talk through it with her. Share what's scary for you and how you plan to handle it.

Becoming a godly woman takes a lifetime!

key point

PATIENCE & KEEPING ON ARE KEY!

If you flip through the TV channels any evening, you'll probably find a show focusing on change. Not change in character or purpose, but change of the physical nature—a man who feels ugly with his deformed teeth is made "whole" following oral surgery, or an obese girl gains confidence as she rapidly sheds pounds. Everything is quick and simple. The message being sent to our girls is: If you're unhappy, change yourself physically, and you'll be happy. And girls believe it! As they compare their bodies and faces to models in magazines, they look for quick fixes to achieve a "perfect" image.

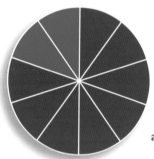

Approximately 8 of 10 teen girls are unhappy with their bodies and want a "quick fix." Remind your teen that the most important changes start on the inside and then are reflected outward.

Our daughters need to understand that positive change takes time and patience. Structures that have stood the test of time were not overnight sensations. The ultimate example is the Sistine Chapel. For eight painful years, Michelangelo climbed the rickety scaffolding to paint, piece by piece, the huge chapel ceiling. He understood that great works of art take a lot of time. The same is true with the incredible creation of a godly woman. Each day, God is adding depth, blending colors, and adding to the work of art!

Remind your daughter that, with patience and perseverance, she can climb any mountain!

Today's kids have no idea what it's like to live without microwaves, cell phones, instant cash, online shopping, or laptops. In this instant world, we need to be teaching (and living) the value of "great things take time."

The big, theological word for this process is *sanctification*. Unlike justification, the act of Jesus stepping in on a sinner's behalf (which happens once in our lives), sanctification takes place from the time we are justified until we are brought into the presence of the Lord.

As much as we'd like a quick fix, we would not be able to handle being sanctified all at once. Over time, God molds and shapes us to look, act, love, and respond more like him. A godly girl embraces the love and attention of her Creator as she is molded in his image.

Middle-school kids can't wait to get older! They see older siblings dating, driving, and staying out late, and they want to be there, too. Help your daughter see the value of being 13 and how having patience to grow older is worth the wait!

Parents have great opportunities to help in the process of molding and shaping. If you're helping your daughter make better choices about friends, don't expect her to abandon her current social group and enter another within twenty-four hours. Instead, affirm her good choices and be patient. If she pushes you away, understand that she desperately needs and wants your attention and instruction—it just hurts to be pruned.

key point
BECOMING A GODLY PERSON IS A PROCESS.

Godly Qualities

When we see a brilliant painting, the first question we ask is: "Who painted this?" Wouldn't it be wonderful if a young woman's qualities were so brilliant that others would exclaim, "Who is responsible for this incredible girl?" We'd know the answer. The One responsible is the One whose character and qualities that young woman reflects!

The body is valuable to God.

When is the last time you stared at your hand simply to marvel at its functionality, intricacy, and flexibility? God made our bodies incredibly—and they are his precious possessions. In a world where we're taught that our bodies are our own, girls need to be reminded whom they belong to.

She needs to know the body God gave her.

I remember playing with my Barbie doll and braiding her long hair. I can't remember when I first became aware that my body looked nothing like Barbie's. Actually, Barbie's body didn't look like my mom, any of the ladies in my church, or my teacher, Miss Williams. Even though the evidence was stacked against Barbie, I found myself wishing I could look like her. I'm thankful my wish never came true. Studies show that if Barbie's measurements were put into human form, she would not be able to stand—she would fall over due to her disproportionate body!

God created girls with a variety of body types— not with unrealistic cookie-cutter shapes!

One of the most important truths for a girl to understand is that God created women with a variety of body types—each with its benefits and beauty. The short, muscular girl will more than likely excel at soccer with her low center of gravity and strong calves. The tall, lean girl has her pick of size-10 shoes and could make a graceful dancer or pianist. You get the idea. So often, however, girls see one body type as the ultimate goal and beat themselves up (sometimes literally) trying to reach that goal. When a girl is able to accept and celebrate her body type, she is able to utilize its benefits for God's glory and her satisfaction.

Even though girls have been warned about developmental changes in their physical bodies, not much can prepare them for the real thing. Its one thing to see pubic hair increasing on outlined bodies in a textbook, but it's completely different to see it in the mirror! We need to be in conversations with girls about their bodies, from a young age, to normalize the changes that seem so drastic.

STOP & CONSIDER

❖ **How did I feel about the physical changes of puberty?**

❖ **How can I help my daughter see the benefits of her body type?**

❖ **How can I initiate a conversation with her about development?**

AGES OF FEMALE PUBERTY IN THE U.S.

14.5 YEARS	13 YEARS	11.7 YEARS
PRE-1900	1900-1970	1971-2005

From: *Hurt* (Chap Clark, 2005)

The average age of female puberty has dropped to just shy of 12 since 1970. Although girls' bodies are maturing more quickly, their minds aren't ready to process all the changes early maturation brings. We must be willing to initiate conversations if we want them to walk through these stages successfully.

THE BODY IS VALUABLE TO GOD.

She needs to care for her body.

key point
PROVIDE HEALTHY FOOD OPTIONS.

During this growing time in her life, a girl needs food—and more than just ice cream and chips! With the exception of infancy, this is the fastest progression of growth a girl will experience in her lifetime. Obviously, food options are endless—and tension lies in the desire girls have to be thin yet eat what they desire. Help your daughter make good food choices by encouraging balanced meals and filling the cupboards with healthy, on-the-go options such as cereal and granola bars.

Many teens reject good carbs and calories to achieve weight goals. The result? Bodies craving the calcium, fat, and calories they need to grow!

During adolescence, 15% of adult height, 50% of adult body weight, and 45% of adult skeletal mass are gained. According to the USDA, 9 of 10 teen girls fail to meet daily calcium requirements. Help your teen choose foods to support her body's changing needs!

When I was in late elementary school, a toy company came out with the "Get in Shape Girl!" set—complete with a headband, hand weights, and cassette tape. It was revolutionary! Girls have so many more opportunities for activity during this sports-saturated time. Whether it's dance, lacrosse, synchronized swimming, softball, or hockey, our girls are more active than any generation before them. The big question is: *Are they healthy?*

key point
EXERCISE IS A KEY TO FEMALE FITNESS!

So often girls see the immediate results of weight loss when they begin to work out with a sport, and training moves into an obsession. Food and exercise go hand in hand: Is she eating enough calories to offset all the activity in her life? Depending on how active they are, teen athletes may need from 2,000 to 5,000 calories per day to meet energy needs!

key point
ATHLETES NEED EXTRA CALORIES.

IT'S A PROBLEM OF PERCEPTION!

40%
9- to 10-year-olds

53%
13-year-olds

78%
17-year-olds

Many young girls are unhappy with their bodies when compared to the images they see in the media. What messages is your daughter receiving, and how can you help her be comfortable in the body God gave her?

Approximately 90-95% of anorexia nervosa sufferers are girls and women.

As a young girl matures, she needs to be attentive to more than just her appearance. Most girls naturally take care of themselves—in fact, some would say they pay too much attention to their personal hygiene! Some girls, however, aren't as motivated and need accountability. The thousands of dollars you have spent on braces and retainers could be in vain if your daughter neglects her teeth. Acne is another concern for teens and parents. Be sure your daughter washes her face daily (but not too much), and if she uses lotions or makeup, look for ones that are *noncomedogenic* or *nonacnegenic*, which means they don't clog pores.

Modest is hottest!

key point
A GIRL'S BODY IS NOT HER ASSET.

I walk through stores each spring and my heart sinks. "Are you serious?" I think, as I lift up the latest string bikini option for our teen-age girls. Society has sold a lie to our girls that their bodies are to be used as assets, to be flaunted and used for their personal gain—and they're falling for it. In droves, girls buy short skirts, low-riding jeans, push-up bras, and lacy thongs. The end results of living that lie are girls with surface esteem, guys who lust after those girls, and a degradation of woman that hurts God's heart.

key point
GUYS PREFER NATURAL GIRLS!

"BEAUTY IS ONLY SKIN DEEP."

Discuss this saying with your teen. Then make a list of what constitutes true beauty in a person.

Back in the mid 1980s, one company created a makeup line for young girls. I was able to convince my Nana Grayce to buy me the complete set one weekend and applied it just before my mom planned to deliver me to my fourth-grade Sunday school class. Let's just say I didn't get to experience the flannelgraph lesson that day! I saw my mom's response as extreme, but I am so thankful for the lesson she taught me that day about moderation. To this day, I sport lipstick and a little bit of powder for my shiny nose—saving a lot of money and allowing others to see the beauty God created in my face. Remind your teen that a little makeup goes a long way!

I am certain the biggest motivator in a girl's "getting ready" process is the attention of guys. They think: *How can I be noticed? Will he like this outfit?* The crazy thing is, guys are not necessarily impressed by the end results. I know because I ask the boys. They hate it when girls cake on makeup and spend so much time on their hair. As Christian guys trying to deny the temptation of lust, they get frustrated with girls who wear low-riding jeans with thongs showing. They're attracted to girls who can look natural and wear jeans, a T-shirt, and a ponytail out the back of a baseball cap.

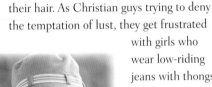

BIG BIBLE POINT

Read I Corinthians 6:19, 20 with your daughter. Discuss how we can live out being "bought at a price" with regard to modesty.

TAKE 5

* How do you show modesty?
* Why is it hard to help your daughter dress modestly?
* Why is it good for your daughter to dress modestly?
* What does modesty say about your daughter?
* How do we honor God through modesty?

For girls who are serious about being modest, some "secret weapons" exist in their battle against society's immodest attack. Can't find a shirt that completely covers her midriff? Buy a shorter shirt and simply add a white tank or T-shirt underneath. When she reaches up into her locker, all that is seen is the secret weapon—not skin! Another great defensive move is layering. If a tank top is showing a little too much skin, just add another layer to cover the exposed area.

✓ MIDDLE-SCHOOL MEMOS

This is the time when girls start to experiment with makeup. Walk through the process with your daughter. Get a makeover together. Talk honestly about how makeup looks on her.

The heart reflects God's love.

Not only did God make our hearts the center of our physical bodies, supplying lifeblood to all areas of our bodies, but he made our spiritual hearts central to our relationships with him. Because of its importance, we need to protect, nurture, and care for our hearts. As our girls walk through daily distractions, let's keep them focused on the heart of the matter.

Comparison is one of Satan's tools.

key point

TEENS TEND TO COMPARE EACH OTHER.

The Bible tells us that Satan is real, crafty, and destructive. In the life of a teenage girl, Satan loves to use the tool of comparison. He knows teen girls' tendency to compare themselves to others. As girls walk into a room, they are tempted to compare and contrast themselves to other girls in the room, asking themselves: *Is she cuter than me? Does she get more attention from boys? Do I look fat compared to her? Is she more athletic?*

key point

"PERFECT" GIRLS ARE NOT PERFECT!

BIG BIBLE POINT

Read John 10:10 with your daughter. Brainstorm the ways Satan attempts to "steal and kill and destroy" in the lives of teenage girls.

What girls don't understand is that the comparison game can never be won. A girl may be able to evaluate herself as more popular than another girl, but there will be a girl more popular still! No matter how hard she tries, there will always be *someone* better—someone skinnier, smarter, stronger, or more popular. And Satan only laughs as each moment a girl spends in the comparison game is a moment gone from pursuing God's incredible plan for her life.

Here's a classic example of the comparison game: A teenage girl walks through the checkout line at the grocery store and picks up the latest glamour magazine. She studies the "perfect" model on the front cover and concludes: *She is beautiful. I don't look like her. I'm not beautiful.* Time out! The truth is that the photo of the "perfect" model has been altered and manipulated through a process called airbrushing. All blemishes— zits, extra flab, unwanted hair, small chest—have been removed or enhanced. The result? Perfection … but not reality.

TARGET MOMENT

Be careful not to play the comparison game with co-workers, neighbors, aerobic instructors, or "perfect" relatives. Remember: Your daughter is watching!

TRY THIS!

Hop on the Internet and search the words "celebrities without makeup" to find examples of celebrities' "before" and "after" pictures. Talk with your daughter about the truth of airbrushing and the made-up people we often compare ourselves to.

Ask your teenage daughter to tell you three things she truly likes about herself, things special to her and not as a comparison to her friends. If she struggles to highlight the positives, affirm those features or qualities as God-given. Then ask, "What's one thing you'd change about yourself if you could and why?" Talk through her ideas, then remind your daughter that God made her in special ways that are uniquely hers!

Comparisons lead to gossip—both are unattractive in teen girls!

"When nobody around you seems to measure up, it's time to check your yardstick."—Bill Lemley

Serving changes hearts!

key point
SERVING EXPRESSES FAITH AND LOVE!

When Jesus got down on his knees before his disciples with basin and towel in hand, they were blown away! He was their leader—they were supposed to serve him! Instead, Jesus gently washed their feet and set a perfect example of serving for his disciples and for us. After Jesus washed the last foot, he told his disciples to wash one another's feet. Jesus could have simply told his friends they needed to serve one another, even ordered them to serve—but he knew they needed to *experience* it.

key point
FOCUS ON OTHERS— FOCUS ON GOD.

"Serve one **another** in **love."**
(Galatians 5:13)

DID YOU KNOW...

80% of evangelical Christians have shared their faith with a non-Christian in the past year. (The Barna Group)

Each July, our junior-high teens engage in a local missions opportunity. We move into a mobile trailer park (sleeping in pop-up trailers and motor homes) and minister to the children living within the community. Each day, kids from the park flock to our VBS program, led by the teens, to hear about Jesus. We play, carry them around, share our lunches, and walk them home late in the evening. This five-day experience changes the lives of every person involved! Junior highers realize what it feels like to be a servant—and experience the energy, love, passion, and life it produces. The kids experience Christ's love as they interact with the teens and watch their every move.

This is the greatest time to get your teen involved in serving! Teens have more time and energy than at any time in their lives. Encourage serving and set a pattern and priority for life! Consider these places for your teen to offer her time and talents!

AT SCHOOL

AT CHURCH

COMMUNITY HELP

IN YOUR FAMILY

LOCAL CHARITIES

It goes against teen nature to be focused on others—they tend to be more self-focused. However, because each teen is a child of God, created in the image of him, each has a true servant's heart. It might need to be dusted off a bit, but it's there! As I interact with adults, I find they set the bar too low for teenagers. Teens are capable of so much more than we give them credit for! I have found that our teens thrive in the midst of serving, often putting adult servants to shame!

DON'T FORGET!
Sharing your faith with others is also serving—and can change hearts and lives forever!

We read in 1 John 4:12 that *"if we love one another, God lives in us and his love is made complete in us."* One of the greatest ways we express love is by serving. In a world where most live for themselves, it's surprising and refreshing to see people humbly serving one another—especially when teens are doing the serving! Each time a girl serves and makes God's love complete will spur her on to serve more. Soon it becomes second nature—and God's love shines brightly!

key point
TEENS CAN CHANGE THE WORLD!

If your daughter can serve in the area of her passion, she will thrive.

Contentment is key to a life of freedom.

Most kids long to be older than they are. Kindergartners can't wait until they're in first grade and go to school all day. The junior higher longs to be in senior high with a driver's license and a later curfew. At the same time, the senior in high school anticipates the freedom and excitement of college. Sadly, we're not much more contented as adults.

Most kids and teens long to be older—and more grown-up.

> *key point*
> **BEING CONTENTED IS A GOD GIFT!**

> **"Trust in the LORD and do good; dwell in the land and enjoy safe pasture" (Psalm 37:3).**

I believe David, the shepherd, is communicating a much-needed message with his words. Picture yourself in a pasture with a fence safely creating a circle around you. This is your current pasture of life. But in our discontentment, we're tempted to move toward the fence and look at others' pastures. We compare pastures and often long to be in another. Sometimes we even try to dig out under the fence or break through with brute strength. We have a hard time simply dwelling.

> **"It is a wise person who knows that the contented person is never poor, while the discontented one is never rich."**
> **—Frank Herbert**

Now, let's put a teenage girl in the middle of her pasture. In the depths of her soul, she may want to dwell in that place, to find contentment in who she is, but everything around her tells her to look for a way out. She needs a boyfriend. She should lose some weight. She should take harder classes. She should get a job to make money to spend on things. She should experiment with drinking. As she leans against the fence, her back to her pasture, the Shepherd is calling to her: "Turn around. I have so much for you to see and experience here!" When she chooses to dwell there, she finds a contentment others cannot understand. And when the Lord chooses to swing the gate of her pasture open, she is able to walk through it with confidence, knowing she enjoyed each moment God intended for her.

BIG BIBLE POINT

Share Psalm 37:3, 4 with your daughter. Then discuss these questions about contentment.

- Where does true joy come from?

- Why does God want us to be contented with him?

- How does trusting God help us be contented?

HOT-TOPIC STARTERS

Who is the most contented person you know? Why?

In what area of your life are you most contented?

What can you do to be more contented?

Some people equate contentment with stagnancy. This misconception highlights the need to be driven and moving forward. The cool thing about God-given contentment is that, as we are dwelling in the pastures of life, God is shaping us to be more like him and moving us along in the journeys he has planned for us. What a great place to be!

Getting better, not bitter, is God's plan.

A classic distinction between guys and girls is that when guys get mad, they hit something and let it go. Girls, however, get mad, talk to other girls about it, and get bitter. Rather than letting it go, girls often take bitterness to the grave. Although some experts say this is simply a natural, unchangeable attribute of females, I disagree. When the fruit of the Spirit (Galatians 5:22, 23) is present, bitterness cannot be found. In the love chapter of 1 Corinthians 13, Paul lists the polar opposites of bitterness when he writes that love does not envy, is not self-seeking or easily angered, and keeps no record of wrong.

> **key point**
> **LOVE DEFEATS BITTERNESS!**

Most girls have a story of hurt in their relational histories. For one girl, a friend took advantage of a shared secret and used it as a social weapon. For another, a group of friends rejected her for no apparent reason. For yet another, cruel nicknames were given and repeated throughout elementary school. Each example has the potential of instilling lifelong bitterness in the heart of a young girl. I have met women in their 40s and 50s who are still holding on to bitterness—and the results are disturbing. Many suffer from low self-esteem, depression, weight issues, and a victim mentality toward life. There must be a better way!

BIG BIBLE POINT

Read Luke 23:32-34. Discuss with your daughter the intensity of Jesus' act of forgiveness. What does this passage show us about how we should forgive others?

Girls could learn a lot from how Joseph handled bitterness in the Old Testament. Joseph's brothers were consumed by jealousy, sold him into slavery, and told his father he was dead. If anyone had a right to be bitter, it was Joseph! Instead, he chose to pour his energy into serving God. He decided to get better, not bitter. At the climax of the story, when Joseph's brothers reenter his life, he is faced with a choice: dig up that bitterness and let 'em have it, or forgive them. Joseph chose the way of love—and everyone was blessed because of it!

✔ **MIDDLE-SCHOOL MEMOS**
Remember that middle-school teens are just learning how to navigate this new relational system. Take time to ask questions, validate feelings, and walk them through forgiveness.

Researcher Richard Fitzgibbons cites these benefits to the one who forgives:

DECREASED LEVELS OF ANGER AND HOSTILITY

IMPROVED PHYSICAL HEALTH

ENHANCED CAPACITY TO TRUST

INCREASED FEELINGS OF LOVE

IMPROVED ABILITY TO CONTROL ANGER

FREEDOM FROM EVENTS OF THE PAST

Remind your teen that failure to forgive locks away love—and creates damaging bitterness!

One of the most important steps in turning bitterness into a better life is forgiveness. Colossians 3:13 says, *"Bear with each other and forgive whatever grievances you may have against one another. Forgive as the Lord forgave you."* For girls, the greatest challenge comes in forgiving and not revisiting the situation. With the Lord's help—and some guidance from adults who care—they can do it!

Perspective changes everything.

When golfer Tiger Woods wants to focus on his putting, he cups his hands around his face and looks through the small opening. It's effective—but only in the game of golf. In the real, Christian life, our hands need to be pulled *away* from our faces so that we can see the broad horizon of God's plan for our lives.

The world is bigger than homeroom.

As a student sits in her homeroom class, the world as she knows it is very small. The teacher and the other students are the players on a small stage, acting out the play of life. So, when midterms are passed out and she has a B-minus, life seems tragic. Granted, some of this smallness is natural in this stage of teen development, but some of it is not. Some of it will follow her into adulthood and make for an incredibly limited perspective on life.

key point
PERSPECTIVE CHANGES EVERYTHING!

TRY THIS!

Encourage your daughter to broaden her perspective by starting with your family. Don't get upset because the neighbor blew leaves into your yard. Sponsor a child together. Give one year's Christmas money toward building a school in Africa.

When I listen to the conversations of average teenage girls, I am often disappointed. They bounce from the topic of boys to shoes to hairspray to nail polish and back to boys again. I understand issues of development and the constant battle of selfishness, but it's still disappointing.

Real sadness sets in when I watch video footage from the International Justice Mission showing young teenage girls being brought out from a cellar with torn clothes, covering their eyes from the bright sun. They are being rescued from child prostitution that's running rampant in many countries. It puts the pressures and concerns of life into perspective. We need to pass that perspective on to our girls.

TARGET MOMENT

During a nonemotional moment, talk with your daughter about what it means to have a kingdom perspective and how it keeps us focused.

If your teen loves animals, have her check out Heifer International at www.heifer.org!

Check out these great sites for opportunities for teens to broaden your teen's world perspective on life:

* International Justice Mission (www.ijm.org)
* One Life Revolution (domino-201.worldvision.org/)
* Compassion International (www.compassion.com)

When your daughter is upset about something that is very "small world-ish," walk through these steps to gain perspective!

1 *Listen* to what she says.

2 *Validate* her feelings.

3 *Ask,* "How bad is this if we have a kingdom perspective?"

Jesus was constantly encouraging others to gain a kingdom perspective. Jesus always wanted people to see more of the plan, the purpose, the perspective. Our teenage daughters need to have their perspectives broadened. The results will bless many, and the benefits will spill over into eternity.

God's plan is bigger than we are.

key point

TEENS CAN BE USED BY THE HOLY SPIRIT.

key point

UTILIZE GIFTS WITH HUMILITY.

The Bible assures us that when we commit our lives to Christ, the Holy Spirit administers at least one spiritual gift to each of us. Even though the Holy Spirit doesn't discriminate due to age, we seem to. When I approach one of my young teen girls about a spiritual gift I see evidenced in her life, my comments are typically met by confusion. Many aren't aware of this promise of Scripture, but even more seem shocked that they are included in the gift-giving as a teenager. I have developed a passion to expose teenagers to the truth of spiritual gifts and give them multiple opportunities to use them.

Because the idea of the body of Christ is such an abstract concept, I intentionally make the idea come alive to kids—and you can do the same with your daughter. Read excerpts from 1 Corinthians 12, introducing the "one body with many parts" plan. Next, unveil a "live model" for the teaching session using a Mr. Potato Head doll. Hold up each piece and assign it a gift. Mr. Potato Head's lips are the gift of prophecy, his ears are mercy, his hands are for helping, and his feet are leadership. Place the pieces in their proper places. To illustrate the importance of each of us ministering where we are gifted, switch the parts around and give Mr. P. the chance to stand. He falls over!

Challenge your daughter to make a "gift list" of the gifts she recognizes in herself. Write the gifts on gift tags and tape them around her mirror as reminders of God's great grace in her life!

MIDDLE-SCHOOL MEMOS

It's natural for a middle schooler to be somewhat self-conscious. As you identify her gifts, give her small, nonpublic ways to use them. As she gains confidence, her self-consciousness will recede.

In a performance-based society, it would be easy for your teen to take pride in her spiritual gifts, especially if she is affirmed in how she uses them. Encourage and affirm the spiritual gifts in your daughter's life. Point out the gift-edness of others, and talk about how we *all* need each other in order to function in the body of Christ.

SERVE OTHERS THROUGH GOD'S SPIRIT!

STOP & CONSIDER

❖ Am I aware of my own gifts?

❖ Do I utilize those gifts?

❖ How can I encourage my daughter to use her gifts?

PROPHESYING

SERVING

TEACHING

ENCOURAGING

LEADING

GIVING

SHOWING MERCY

As your daughter humbly discovers her spiritual gifts, she will begin to see the scope of God's plans. She will also discover that she doesn't have to be perfect. Where she lacks, another person in the body excels. When she makes a poor decision or steps out of God's will, the plan doesn't fall apart. She plays a vital role, but the body and the plan compensate for her weaknesses.

We may be the only Jesus they see.

When I was a senior in high school, a girl named Teresa handed me her senior picture as we opened our side-by-side lockers. I thanked her and flipped over the picture as she walked away. Teresa had written, "Heather, thank you for saying hi to me. Sometimes it was the only thing that got me through the day." I was blown away! I truly had an acquaintance-like relationship with Teresa. We never hung out on the weekends or ate lunch together. Yet my simple greeting each day meant the world to her.

key point
KINDNESS CAN CHANGE LIVES!

Our faith and love for the Lord should inspire us to reach out to others and love them in his name.

key point
LOVE OTHERS — LOVE JESUS.

If your daughter needs to be convinced of her role as being Christ-like to others, point her to Matthew 25:31-46. Here Jesus describes the events of the final days and explains how people will be separated into two groups—the goats and the sheep. Those who loved, fed, visited, and cared for others will be considered righteous and humbly accept the label of *sheep*. Those, however, who ignored prisoners, turned away the hungry, and left others cold and naked will be called *goats* and will be separated from the righteous. I want to be with the sheep!

BIG BIBLE POINT

Read John 15:5. Talk about the kind of fruit that naturally flows from you as you hold to the Vine. What fruit only comes when you cling to the Vine and bank on the power of Christ?

When you find your daughter exuding kindness, immediately follow it up with affirmations such as, "I can see Christ's love in you!"

One way teenage girls can be godly is to be *kind*. Sounds simple, but genuine kindness in today's society is powerful—and rare. How does she treat the kid sitting alone day after day in the lunchroom? How does she respond when someone accuses her of doing something she didn't do? Walking though her day, your daughter has many opportunities to offer kindness. If she merely responds to *one* of these, she could change a life. The great thing about kindness is that it's in our DNA!

Another area girls can focus on as they love others is *sacrifice*. Imagine your daughter offering to help another student with his project or being the first to volunteer when the coach says, "Who'd be willing to sit out this quarter?" People will notice and ask, "What's different about her?" We know what's different.

Being created in the image of God, we have his qualities instilled in us. It's just a matter of tapping into that kindness.

Your daughter is watching you! How do you respond to a knock at the door during supper? How many times a day do you choose to be kind, even if it's not convenient? You are a living textbook— let her read you!

Earthly Dangers

As a girl walks through a typical day, she is bombarded with messages. Some resemble truth, but many are dangerous myths or outright lies. Due to the repetitive nature of the messages, even the most levelheaded of girls may begin to be drawn in. How do we help our girls discern these messages and respond in healthy ways?

Self-worth shouldn't come from looks.

From infancy, a girl's physical appearance is noticed, then either affirmed or critiqued. Although affirmation is essential in the formation of a young girl's self-esteem, we need to be sure we're affirming the most important things.

Our bodies were bought at a price.

Paul writes in 1 Corinthians 6:19, 20 that our bodies were bought for a price. The powerful truth that our bodies are not our own gets drowned out by the voices of teen idols. Britney Spears and Jessica Simpson, in multiple interviews over the years, have intimated that they've worked hard for their bodies—and can do whatever they want with them.

key point
OUR BODIES BELONG TO GOD.

"You are not your own; you were bought at a price. Therefore, honor God with your body" (1 Corinthians 6:19, 20).

Help your teen to realize that God sent his Son to die the most painful death ever known to humankind in order to save us from being slaves to the world and finding value in ourselves. A grateful heart should lead us to treat our bodies with respect and seek to honor God in every way we use them. If our girls can grasp the knowledge of this loving ownership, it will change their perspectives, relationships, fashion choices, and, ultimately, their lives.

Girls naturally desire to dress more modestly when they know that God owns their bodies!

BIG BIBLE POINT

Read Zephaniah 3:17 with your daughter, then discuss why God takes delight in her and rejoices over her. Is God celebrating her outward or inward person? Why?

When a girl realizes the price that was paid for her body, she begins to care about how her body is being displayed, cared for, and looked at. I have personally seen conviction lead girls to stand in front of their closets and pull out hanger after hanger of clothing they now see as immodest and ungodly. They take more time in front of the mirror (is that possible?) discerning whether or not their outfits are appropriate. Although laying down guidelines is important, those rules need to have godly support behind them or they will be left at the doorstep as our girls leave for college.

MIDDLE-SCHOOL MEMOS **Fashion drive revs up at the onset of middle school. Be sure to set clear, godly boundaries in clothing choices!**

A girl's body continues to change.

Remember your teen days when those jeans were baggy on your little frame and when your skin was tight and unblemished? All of us wish those days could have extended throughout our lives—but they don't. Harshly, our bodies change. For women, the changes seem drastic. Most young girls cannot even fathom stretch marks and wide hips. They hop from store to store purchasing low-riding jeans and cropped tops, never imagining things will change. But things *will* change, and if a girl's worth is tied to her appearance, a crisis is looming in her future.

key point
CHANGES ARE NATURAL— AND CERTAIN.

My childhood friend Amy was the target of jealousy during my early teen years. She could consume a pizza and not gain an ounce! She was lean, small-chested, and could run for miles. I, on the other hand, started wearing a bra in the fourth grade and seemed to gain five pounds when I even smelled a pizza! Amy loved her body type and all the benefits it gave her. But in eighth grade, everything changed. Almost overnight, Amy developed hips. Not just average hips, but wide, hard-to-find-jeans-that-fit hips. Amy struggled with the changes in her body. Could her experience have been better or at least softened a bit? I think so!

key point
CHANGE IS PART OF GOD'S PLAN, TOO.

Helping girls in this area is all about balance! If we spend too much time drawing a picture filled with wrinkles, sagginess, and thinning hair, we'll cause them to fear and dread maturing. However, if we ignore the truths of aging completely, we're setting them up for a shock at age 35!

Help your teen recognize beauty at *any* age!

TRY THIS!

Moms, take out your photographs and choose one from each life stage. Lay them out on the table and talk honestly with your daughter about the changes in your body and how those changes made you feel. It's okay—and even helpful—to acknowledge the wrinkles around your eyes or the difficulty you have losing weight now that you're a bit older.

When you're shopping with your daughter, highlight the positive by saying, "That shirt flatters your shape" or "God gave you a great build!"

God created women's bodies differently than guys' bodies. We have wider hips, the right anatomy, and innate maternal instinct to set us up perfectly to bear children. During that time, our bodies change significantly—all to house, protect, and deliver the baby growing inside. It's a miracle! Yet recent female-targeted magazines boast headlines such as "Body After Baby: Stars Share Secrets of Their Amazing Slimdowns!" No matter the miracle, society's focus always seems to come back to the body. We need to help our girls understand that there is so much more to life than having the "ideal" body!

MIDDLE-SCHOOL MEMOS

Most middle-school girls are smack in the middle of body changes! Some feel inadequate, others too developed. Help your daughter through this time by talking, sharing, asking questions—and being available!

Girls must give their bodies what's needed.

key point
HEALTHY CHOICES ARE A PRIORITY.

As a young girl grows, her body needs more— more sleep, more of the right foods, more movement, and more attention. The tension here is that the need for more comes with the desire for more independence. When kids are younger, parents can more easily control eating and sleeping routines. Not so with teens! With many teens working and participating in so many activities, parents have less of a direct influence on the care of their

Researchers at Stanford University held a Summer Sleep Camp, where they monitored the sleeping patterns of preadolescent kids through their teen years. They discovered that teens require more sleep—somewhere between one and two hours more—than their 10-year-old siblings. However, most teenagers get one to two hours less!

30% of teenagers are employed for more than 20 hours weekly and have more symptoms of daytime sleepiness than those who don't work. (*Boston Globe*)

DID YOU KNOW ...

Our adolescent children are the sleepiest members of society. This sleepiness is associated with poor school performance, drug and alcohol use, and increased automobile accidents.

key point
MAKE GOOD CHOICES FOR YOUR BODY.

Physical inactivity is a major risk factor for developing coronary artery disease, high blood pressure, and obesity. The American Heart Association recommends at least 60 minutes of moderate physical activity every day for kids and teens. Activity produces overall physical, psychological, spiritual, and social benefits. But as your daughter increases her activity level, be sure she increases her water intake!

Keep a gentle eye on your daughter to be sure she is living a healthy eating life. The symptoms of anorexia nervosa (starving one's body) are as follows:

WEIGHT AT 85% OR LESS THAN NORMAL

INTENSE FEAR OF WEIGHT GAIN

DISTORTED BODY IMAGE

LOSS OF THREE CONSECUTIVE PERIODS

BIG BIBLE POINT

Read Matthew 6:25–34 with your daughter. Discuss how we can live the truth of this passage and yet be sure we're living healthy lives. List ways we can honor God by making healthy choices each day.

One of the most harmful ways girls mistreat their bodies is through eating disorders that are coping mechanisms for lives that feel out of control. The most common disorders are *anorexia nervosa* (an intense and irrational fear of gaining weight) and *bulimia nervosa* (cycles of binge eating and purging). They are sometimes deadly conditions that need to be approached and treated—but with great care.

Our nation has an obsession with food and dieting, with Americans spending over $40 billion on diet-related products each year!

Inner beauty is the most attractive.

key point

BEAUTY SHOULD COME FROM THE HEART.

In 1 Peter 3:3, 4 we're told that beauty is not to be an outward adornment but to radiate from the *inside*. I love how the truth of this Scripture is meant for girls today, too! The majority of what is marketed toward young girls is related to outward appearances—fashion, romantic relationships, makeup, and physical appearance. As is typically his way, God bucks the popular trends with his Word. If girls shift their focus to inner beauty, they're assured of its longevity—and of the Lord's pleasure!

Mirror, mirror, on the wall—whose HEART is fairest of them all?

Write verses such as 1 Peter 3:3, 4 on colorful note cards and tape them to your daughter's bathroom mirror. When her morning routine calls her to focus on the outer beauty, she can focus on her inner beauty as well.

Some girls who fall in the extroverted and talkative sector of the personality scale may be put off by this verse. I believe what the author was getting at here was not an issue of the mouth but an issue of the heart. That talkative girl should ask herself these questions: "How do I respond to people who are hurting? Do I react with a calm spirit? When I approach a conflict, do I do it with a gentle and loving attitude?" Her answers are a good gauge as to whether, despite her exuberant nature, she is heading in the right direction.

"God saw all that he had made, and it was very good" (Genesis 1:31). Remind your daughter that God doesn't make junk—he loves her as she is inside—not just outside!

One reason people are drawn to girls with inner beauty is because they offer steadiness in the midst of chaos and inconsistency. As teens walk through a typical day, they never know what they may encounter. Someone who was loyal yesterday could completely turn on her friend today because she didn't call last night. His social group might decide that everyone in the group needs to drink. Enter stage right, a girl who is even-tempered, consistent, loving, kind, unassuming, and gentle. Peers are curious and attracted to what they know is different and real.

Teens in middle or high school set patterns of behavior that carry through the rest of their lives. Help create a balanced focus on her inner *and* outer beauty!

TAKE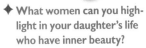

+ What women can you highlight in your daughter's life who have inner beauty?

+ How much money does your family spend on outer versus inner resources?

+ Does your daughter observe a quiet and gentle spirit in you or other role models?

+ How do you express your own inner beauty?

+ How can you help your daughter develop a godly spirit and inner beauty?

key point

INNER BEAUTY NEVER FADES.

In the Bible we read that Esther was known for her natural beauty. Her true beauty, however, was revealed when she chose to step up, regardless of the cost, to protect those who couldn't protect themselves. Her legacy is one of the heart, not of the body. In youth ministry, I've had the honor of interacting with girls who chose to focus on inner rather than outer beauty. Megan was magnetic. She initiated conversations with new kids, had compassion, and loved the Lord. People were always drawn to the inner beauty of Megan!

Self-worth shouldn't come from guys.

The average teenage girl may agree with this statement—but she probably *feels* differently! It may seem to her as if everyone who is anyone has a boyfriend. Even the most grounded girls feel the pressure to be in a relationship. How can we help our girls understand that self-worth isn't about guys or having boyfriends?

We're created to be in relationships.

key point
GOD CREATED RELATIONSHIPS.

Although the word *trinity* is not found in the Bible, plenty of verses proclaim the truth that God is three-in-one: Father, Son, and Holy Spirit. It's impossible for our minds to comprehend how this works, but one thing we know for sure is that the three are in relationship with one another. God didn't have to have it that way; he *chose* to. I am certain he wanted to give us a pure example of relationship. And since we're all created in the image of God, we are meant to be in relationships as well.

Read Colossians 3:12-14. Discuss how these qualities could be applied to relationships with other girls.

Recent research on the brain has given scientists a new perspective on adolescent development. The prefrontal cortex, located behind the forehead and above the eyebrows, is the part of the brain that governs such things as planning ahead, assessing consequences, and controlling impulses. Until individuals reach their early 20s, this part of the brain is not fully mature. For girls, a new chemical is introduced that causes them to connect physically, emotionally, and relationally with others; hence girls holding hands and sacrificing in order to be in friendships.

Relationships are also essential for girls when it comes to processing life. Whereas boys tend to withdraw and process internally, the typical girl needs to process verbally with another individual. During the early years, her processing partner is often a parent or close sibling. As she enters adolescence, however, she changes partners, choosing to process life with girlfriends. This is why girls can spend the entire weekend together and still spend three hours on the phone with each other once in their respective homes. Adult men will attest to this female need extending through adulthood!

It's not unusual for me to get a phone call from the parent of a seventh-grade boy following a youth retreat. "Heather, I don't know what to do! Since Derek got back, a girl named Kayla has called eleven times! Is this normal?" Unfortunately for that poor mom, it is. Early on, boys engage in the playground game "boys chase girls, then girls chase boys" because of the hunt and victory. Girls play because they truly want to catch the boys or to be caught. The prospect of a relationship, even at that young age, is desirable. Add time, hormones, and opportunity to that and watch out!

TARGET MOMENT

If your daughter becomes interested in a boy, help her draw boundaries in her pursuit of him. Point out that it's more fun to have him call her—then she knows he wants to talk to her.

✔ **CHECK THIS OUT!**

Because of the way the brain is developing, girls often interpret a touch from a boy as a desire for a committed relationship, and boys interpret touch from a girl as a sexual advance. This misinterpretation can lead to harmful things such as hurt feelings, unwanted sex, or damaged reputations.

Biblical math equals number ONE.

When I was in third grade, I learned about fractions. Not being mathematically inclined, I had a hard time catching on. Despite my limitations, I did know that in the mathematical world, ½ + ½ = 1. Many people transfer this same equation to relationships. It is assumed that if I, as an individual with needs and wants (one half), can find a guy who fills those needs and wants (my other "half"), I will have a complete relationship. As a result, people spend a significant part of their lives trying on different matches to see who can cover their weaknesses and fulfill their needs.

If you're looking for someone to complete you, you'll always feel half-empty!

key point
NEEDS CHANGE— SO DO PEOPLE.

Let's talk about needs. As a first grader, I needed to chase boys. I'd run around with multiple targets in my range. As a fifth grader, I didn't chase any longer but had a need to be protected with someone to stand up for me. I could go on, but the point is that my needs changed from day to day and year to year. If a girl seeks to find a young man who fulfills her present needs, what happens when her needs change (and they will) and he doesn't meet them any longer? She moves on to another … and another … and another.

✓ **MIDDLE-SCHOOL MEMOS**

Middle-school girls are setting relationship patterns that often extend throughout life. If she seeks to fulfill her needs through boys now, she will do the same when she's 30. It's vital to shift the focus to the "1" early!

key point

GOD PLANNED FOR RELATIONSHIPS.

The Bible offers a different equation. The creation story informs us that we were created in the image of God—complete and whole. God, however, knew we would desire to be in relationship, as he is with the Trinity. Genesis 2:18 reads: *"The LORD God said, 'It is not good for the man to be alone. I will make a helper suitable for him.'"* At that moment, God took Adam, being whole, and joined him with Eve, one who was created in God's image as well. Biblical math was created: 1 + 1 = 1 whole relationship!

1 + 1 = 1 RELATIONSHIP

TRY THIS!

As a family, take a fruit of the Spirit quiz. Using the qualities in Galatians 5:22, 23, rank yourselves on a scale of 1–10 for each. Be honest! Then discuss specific ways you can increase those fruits in your lives.

STOP & CONSIDER

❖ When was a time I tried to meet a need by being with someone else?

❖ How do I focus on being the "1"?

❖ Do I allow God's image to flow unhindered through me?

❖ How can I encourage my daughter to focus on the "1"?

Aside from introducing her to her Savior, one of the most life-giving acts you can do for your daughter is to help her focus on strengthening her "1" rather than looking for a young man to fulfill her needs. Does she reflect God? Is she kind and giving? All of these are in us because they are qualities of God, but they are often hindered by selfishness and sin. However, I've never met a girl who has regretted focusing on being the "1" to glorify God!

Celebrate! God made us whole and complete in his image!

SELF-WORTH SHOULDN'T COME FROM GUYS.

Avoid paper-plate mentalities.

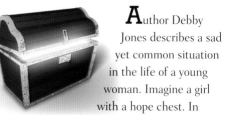 **A**uthor Debby Jones describes a sad yet common situation in the life of a young woman. Imagine a girl with a hope chest. In

key point

USE GOD'S GIFTS TODAY!

the hope chest you'd find china, lace tablecloths, silver spoons, candleholders, and much more. The girl often opens her hope chest and dreams of the day she will marry and use these treasures. Yet each day, this same young woman eats her supper on paper plates at a bare table in a dimly lit room. She's living with a paper-plate mentality. She chooses to live with mediocrity when splendor sits only inches away from her. What a sad way to live!

REACHING FOR THE HEAVENS IS FINE—AS LONG AS YOU SEE THE BEAUTY OF THE STARS TODAY!

Although our teen girls may not be pining away for marriage, they longingly wait for other things. One girl may look forward to the day when she'll feel spiritually mature. She envisions herself using her gifts, being able to quote Scripture, and leading others to Christ. As she looks ahead, the tools she needs are right here waiting for her! All she needs to do is open the chest and throw away the paper plates! Another girl may be setting long-range goals for college and graduate school—and focuses so much that she misses short-term goals that could bring great joy and lead her to future goals!

BIG BIBLE POINT

Read John 10:10. Discuss how the thief attempts to steal a girl's present and future. Ask your daughter, "How are you living life to the fullest right now?" and "How are you honoring God today?"

Paul writes in Ephesians 5:15, 16: *"Be very careful, then, how you live ... making the most of every opportunity, because the days are evil."* These words are not meant to cause fear, but to instill a sense of urgency. We're not promised one more day, let alone another year. Because of this, we need to live life to its fullest and not let any opportunities slip by! We should encourage our teen girls to go for it and seek opportunities to honor God. Student Council. Mission trips. Competitive cheerleading. Leading the worship team. Bring it on!

GOD GAVE YOUR TEEN LIFE—ENCOURAGE HER TO USE IT TO HONOR GOD!

The end result for a girl who denies the paper-plate mentality can be summed up in two words: *no regrets.* When the event she was looking forward to arrives, she can look back at the last years and know that she did not waste one moment. If it was a romantic, godly relationship she looked forward to, she can enter into it with confidence knowing she spent the time leading up to it glorifying God and becoming more like him. If her target was college, she'll realize her four years in high school were filled with opportunities and great memories. Now, that's the way to live!

TARGET MOMENT

As a family, live with the hope chest wide open! Don't wait until vacation to spend time together—do it tonight! Don't wait to share your gifts— do it now!

Many teens turn down the opportunity to be baptized because they think they aren't "good enough" Christians. The tricky part is that they'll never be good enough to deserve God's grace — that's why it's such a gift!

Self-worth shouldn't come from performance.

Life as a girl in today's world is good in so many ways. Unlike generations before, girls aren't limited by their gender. They can organize hockey and lacrosse teams, hold positions of leadership, and don't wear *culottes* to gym class (okay, there is some personal bitterness coming out in that one!). What a great time to be a girl! The downside is the increased pressure to perform. And girls who tend to be people pleasers feel it even more.

Girls' dreams need to be their own.

When a baby is born, most parents, whether they consciously know it or not, have great plans and dreams for their child. Depending on their own interests, parents may envision their daughter or son as a concert pianist, an Olympic gymnast, a missionary, or even the president of the United States!

> **key point**
> GOD DETERMINES THE PLANS!

> **key point**
> PARENTS HAVE HOPES FOR THEIR CHILDREN.

These hopes and aspirations come mostly from love and passion for the small child. Other times, however, the plans come from a parent's own lack of opportunities, failures, or successes in the past. Parents may desire their daughter to have the thrill of victory as they did. Or they may desire their daughter to avoid the shame of not measuring up as they might have. The end result is often disaster.

PARENT POINTER

Teens involved in extracurricular activities are less likely to be involved in drugs, drinking, and other disruptive activities.

Jeremiah 29:11 brings a powerful message to the lives of individuals by telling us that God has plans for us. *Who* has the plans? The Lord has the plans! Yet some parents want to push *their* plans at the expense of the child. I attended a hockey game where two fathers were kicked out of the arena for yelling vulgarities and threats at the refs on the ice. The sons watched as the fathers walked out. Whose dream was each dad pushing?

Wise parents ask themselves: "Whose dream am I supporting?

Teens often feel as if their parents have always been adults and don't understand them. In order to break through that misconception, share with your daughter a time when you had a dream for your life and how you felt as you worked to make that dream a reality.

✦ Did your parents live vicariously through you?

✦ Did you feel supported in your activities by your parents?

✦ How do you support your daughter's dreams?

✦ How do you help her seek God's plans for her life?

Your overwhelming love for your daughter can be put into powerful action when you support her interests and activities—even if you have no natural interest other than her. I have talked with daughters of professional athletes, musicians, and politicians. Some want to follow in the footsteps of their parents; others have no desire to do so. I am continually encouraged and impressed with the parents who say, "That's great, honey! Whatever you want to do, we'll support you!" For the people-pleasing daughter, this message is one of great freedom!

When girls perform for others, no one wins.

I talk with girls a lot. We typically start with fashion, movies, and hair, but I dig deeper as soon as I get the opportunity. As we talk about the activities a girl is involved in, I try to gauge her passion for involvement. Half of the time, a girl will talk forever about how she "lives, eats, and breathes" skating, girls' chorus, hockey, or the flag core. Just watching her talk, I can tell she is passionate and committed. The other half of the time, I hear, "Well, it's okay. I mean, I guess I like it. It's good for me. That's what my mom says" or something along those lines.

key point

BEING INVOLVED IS A HEALTHY THING.

PARENT POINTER

The next time your daughter's report card comes in the mail, before opening it, tell her you love her and celebrate her no matter what is written inside on the report.

Please don't misunderstand me—I am a huge advocate of all extracurricular activities and value the benefit of being a part of a team, learning from other adults, and being competitive. But some teens are involved simply because they don't want to let their parents down—or worse, are fearful of them. Not only does a girl invest a lot of time and energy in something she won't carry into adulthood; she also learns that her worth and love are based on performance.

key point

WHEN GIRLS PERFORM, THEY LOSE THEMSELVES.

As a teenage girl strives to please others through her achievements, she loses herself. She can no longer discern what she wants versus what others want. In order to survive, she has convinced herself that this is what she wants. Years later, she will come to a critical point where she realizes the truth—and years and opportunities will have washed away. As an adult, she will fight the temptation, often for the rest of her life, to please others while denying her own God-given passions and interests.

TARGET MOMENT

It's important to send the message of nonperformance love every day, but be intentional when responding to wins and losses in your child's life.

When a girl performs for others, she forgets where her eternal value comes from. God loves her because he created her. Period. He adores her, protects her, and rejoices over her with song—and it's not a victory song. It's a love song. There is no need to perform or score points with God because he looks beyond the physical to the heart. A girl caught in the performance trap misses this. Even when she walks through the doors of youth group, she carries the same mentality of performance—leading worship, memorizing verses, answering all the questions, and wondering why she still feels so far from God.

"To thine own self be true, and it must follow, as the night the day, thou canst not then be false to any man."
—William Shakespeare

Discuss this famous quote and what it means to be true to yourself and your own dreams. What is the value in being true to yourself? How does this honor God?

Read Daniel 6. Discuss what it would have looked like for Daniel to have performed for others. What was the result when he refused? How was God glorified?

Keep God as your focus!

key point
EVERY GIFT COMES FROM GOD.

key point
GIVE THE PRAISE TO GOD!

It's so fun to watch middle schoolers discover their gifts! For most, their bodies, voices, and thoughts are catching up with their ideas and passions. As they begin to experience success and attention, we need to bring them back to the truth. James 1:16, 17 reminds us that every good gift is from God. This truth combats our sinful tendency to think it's all about us. If our kids can be grounded in this, their futures of glorifying the Lord through their gifts are nearly limitless!

STOP & CONSIDER

❖ Are you performing for an audience of One?

❖ How do you handle praise?

❖ Do you take risks?

❖ How can you encourage your daughter to hear only God's applause?

To stress the importance of focusing on God, I use this example. After reading Galatians 1:10, I bring out a full-length mirror. I acknowledge that it's fun to get compliments from others—it makes us feel good—but if we keep the compliments for ourselves, we're not giving credit to whom it belongs. While I hold the mirror in my hands, I ask a student to give me a compliment. When she finishes, I thank her as I duck behind the mirror, directing the compliment up toward the ceiling to God.

Remind your teen daughter that her talents and gifts come from God and that he is happy when she uses and enjoys them—and thanks him in prayer!

I also teach this truth through volleyball. As I talk about the importance of passing praise to the Lord, I volley the ball back and forth with a student who plays volleyball. I say, "Imagine if I were to catch the volleyball, hold it, and never send it back. That would be selfish. It's the same with praise we receive from others. Certainly we can acknowledge the compliment, but within seconds we need to pass the praise to the One who deserves it. A good response would be, 'Thanks! The Lord just loaned me this skill for my time on earth!'" When we do this, God is glorified and people get a glimpse of who we belong to.

REMIND YOUR TEEN TO "VOLLEY" THE PRAISE BACK TO GOD!

TRY THIS!

Next time you have the family all together, use the mirror or volleyball example to talk about praise. Set a challenge for the whole family—if someone doesn't respond by passing on the praise, he or she can do the dishes!

When a young girl learns her life is played out in front of an audience of One, wonderful things happen. She handles criticism from others, knowing what she did was pleasing to the One who matters. She is free to take risks because she understands her worth is not based on performance. She is less influenced by peer pressure because she knows what the Lord desires of her. Others who watch and hear her response to praise will see she's focused on glorifying the One who gave her these gifts and talents.

Read Psalm 37:4. Talk about what it means to "delight yourself in the LORD." How could this relate to the issue of performance?

Forming Strong Relationships

From the time she's old enough to grasp the arm of a baby doll, a girl attempts to form relationships. She talks giddily about all her friends in her preschool classes and revels in her birthday party when she can invite her closest friends. With the power relationships hold in the lives of our girls, we want to be sure they are choosing and forming strong ones.

Families are a source of strength.

The first opportunity for relationships begins within the family. Moms get a head start in connecting with the daughter, but fathers and siblings are quick to follow suit. If a girl is able to form a steady bond with her family unit at a young age, the relationships that follow will more than likely reflect that same steadiness.

Honor your father and mother.

Although adolescence was not labeled as a life stage when the Lord gave Moses the Ten Commandments, I am certain parents had issues with their children. If they didn't have struggles, God wouldn't have included "Honor your father and mother" and attach a promise of a long life to it. I believe God knew how it would be in the twenty-first century. Portable DVD players, iPods, messages from the media, and the Internet give teenagers more opportunities to isolate and think they are mature beyond their years—disrespecting their parents in the process.

key point
GOD KNOWS WHAT TEENS ARE LIKE.

As children move toward the age of 12, a definite change happens in the parent and child relationship. The daughter who used to make any excuse to sleep in your room—even in your bed—now locks her bedroom door and refuses to be tucked in. Although it's often worrying to parents, these changes in autonomy are natural.

The journey from dependent to independent must happen in order for a child to become a responsible adult.

When your daughter treats you with respect—calling if she'll be late, asking for a ride in advance, and so on—praise her and tell her how much you appreciate being honored and respected.

PARENT POINTER

Parents of middle-school teens often move through life in a state of confusion as their teens become independent. Relax! It's normal. Continue to draw boundaries, encourage them, and pray.

During this journey, it is essential for parents to create *windows*: opportunities to see into the life of your child while allowing her the space she needs. You can create a window by volunteering to work at the information desk for the youth ministry. When you allow your home to be a safe, fun place for her to invite her friends over on weekends, you create a window. These windows allow your daughter to develop naturally yet still honor you.

key point
SHARE TIME WITH YOUR TEEN.

REMEMBER: Positive reinforcement is always a powerful tool!

Blended families are a picture of God's grace.

key point

FAMILIES COME IN MANY SHAPES.

Life as a "traditional" family with teens can be difficult. Add to the normal issues the changes brought about by the blended family, and the results have the potential to be disastrous. You remember the Bradys, don't you? Mike and Carol tried to blend three boys and three girls from opposing families—and it was a challenge! TV's favorite family spent many seasons trying to make it work. Fictitious? Many blended families would say no.

Teens need what all we all need in new situations— time to adjust!

BIG BIBLE POINT

Read Romans 8:28, then discuss the following:

✦ How are God's plans shown through blended families?

✦ Why must we never judge God's plans?

✦ How can we continue to thank God in all things?

Teens moving into a blended situation need time.

Some teens might feel as though they are somehow to blame for their parents breaking up. Others may feel a sense of relief, especially if there was a lot of fighting between parents. Blended families can help healing begin if communication is open and warm!

Some are recovering from a divorce or working through a parent's death. I met with a junior-high girl who lost her father to cancer. I asked, "How would you feel if your mom started dating again?" You'd have thought I had suggested murder! "Never! That will never happen! My mom can't love anyone else but my dad!" This teen has a long way to go before being comfortable with a possible life change in relationships.

TARGET MOMENT

As hard as it may be, it is most helpful for your teen if you to talk early on about dating intentions. Even if relationships don't work, your communication will be helpful!

If you're the stepparent of a teen, understand that your role needs to reflect the emotional place of the teen.

Liz lost her birth mom early in life and hated the fact that her dad was getting married again. She says, "It was never explained well to me. My dad just told me to call her Mom, and I remember being super confused. Debby, my stepmom, was very persistent and consistent, and that helped out a lot. She played with me, let me help her cook, and did my nails. The fact that she loved me unconditionally even though I was horrible to her was what eventually worked." As Liz's stepmom, Debby didn't force her way into the parent role. The end result is a college-age daughter who has an incredible relationship with her stepmom!

> God **works** for the **good** of those who **love** him.
> (Romans 8:28)

It is said that the first year is often the hardest for all family members, but remind your teen that things will settle down and get easier. However, if you find your teen is having trouble adjusting to her new life after your remarriage, consider speaking with your physician or a professional counselor to help her deal with her feelings.

Teen years can be miserable or magnificent.

Although some rebellion is natural during the teen years, constantly pushing limits and buttons is not a healthy pattern. In rebellious kids, boundaries may have been spoken when they were young, but not enforced. The child began to understand she was in control. If she didn't want to sleep in her bed, she'd put up a fuss until she slept on her parents' bedroom floor. If she wanted something in the store, she'd whine until the parent gave in. As insignificant as these individual situations seem, they add up to a teen who believes she controls her life and family.

key point
SET AND STICK TO BOUNDARIES.

Though parents often believe that their daughters are angels, rebellious teens do begin as rebellious kids. Always be consistent, understanding, and in control!

One of the crucial mistakes parents make is choosing to wear the "friend hat" rather than the "parent hat." When parents wear the friend hat, they focus on the fun things of life. Interactions with their teens revolve around shopping, eating out, party hosting, sports, and talking about dating. When it comes to enforcing curfews or reprimanding poor behavior, they tend to back down quickly. Parents who wear the friend hat are inconsistent in their expectations and in following through on punishments.

key point
PARENTS NEED TO WEAR THE PARENT HAT!

It's important for your teen to feel she can trust you and have fun with you—but your primary roles are to guide, protect, direct, mentor, and discipline. Families who are living magnificent lives with teenagers in the house have found a healthy balance in these areas.

> When your daughter seems to be sending the message "Leave me alone!" what she's really saying is, "I need you to understand me!" Don't back off. Gently move toward her because she needs you.

Within my ministry to junior-high girls, I try to help students understand that much of the responsibility of relationships with their parent falls on the girls themselves. They can choose to see their parent as an enemy or as an ally. This choice is the hinge point for the magnificent or miserable experience.

Unfortunately, as the parent, you don't have a lot of control in your daughter's decisions. If your daughter truly sees and treats you like the enemy, lift her up in prayer, asking the Holy Spirit to soften her heart. As you allow the Lord to work, be consistent in holding established boundaries and in your loving attitude toward her. She may not appreciate it right now, but it's what she needs—and truly wants.

STOP & CONSIDER ...

❶ How did your parents set boundaries for you?

❷ In what ways did you respond?

❸ What clear boundaries have you set for your daughter?

❹ Do you follow through with consequences if boundaries are crossed?

It's possible for siblings to be friends.

As much as you may not want to hear it, it's natural for tension to exist between your children. The first siblings ever to walk the earth, Cain and Abel, had some severe rivalry issues. Their sinful natures collided around the altar of the Lord. Cain brought his offering, and Abel brought his. God found favor with Abel's sacrifice, and Cain became insanely jealous. Sound familiar? Despite having parents who had walked and talked with God himself, the boys found reasons to fight.

key point
SIBLING RIVALRY IS VERY COMMON.

key point
NEVER COMPARE YOUR KIDS TO EACH OTHER.

Some parents of elementary-aged children firmly refuse to be involved until the children have tried to resolve the issue in their own ways.

Although middle-school teens often make great babysitters, use your eldest child sparingly as the authoritative figure. The babysitter versus younger sibling matchup can stoke the sibling rivalry fire!

The way you handle and respond to squabbles early on will set the tone for the teen years. One mom challenges her oldest son by saying, "Buddy, as the oldest, you need to be the one in charge. You need to do whatever it takes to be a part of the solution." When more is needed, they talk about Philippians 2:3, 4, which encourages us to consider others before ourselves.

Much of sibling tension is *seasonal*. When my sister, Faith, and I were three years apart in high school, things were often volatile. When I was a freshman, I wanted to wear her sweatshirt. You'd have thought I was asking her to donate her big hair to science! We could argue for 15 minutes about one piece of clothing! I remember my parents being so frustrated with us. But something changed the summer before Faith left for college. She would almost daily ask me to hang out with her. Her freshman year at college was filled with multiple visits and phone calls. To this day, that kind of relationship has continued and deepened. We made it through the season!

"Comparison is a death knell to sibling harmony."
—Elizabeth Fishel

BIG BIBLE POINT

Read I John 4:7-12 together and discuss how these verses relate to relationships with our siblings, parents, and other family members. End with a prayer asking God to remind you of loving all family members.

CONSIDER THIS…

✦ **What was your relationship like with siblings or cousins when you were a child?**

✦ **Did your relationships move through seasons?**

✦ **How do you encourage your children's relationships with siblings or family members?**

✦ **How can you use tense seasons as teachable moments?**

One of the most life-giving things parents can do is to celebrate the differences of each child. Imagine a family with two girls. One is brilliant in science, math, and philosophy. The other excels in the arts. As easy as it would be to think, "I wish my artistic child could be more conscientious and organized like my other child," you need to resist that temptation. Kids need to know they're celebrated for who they are—not compared to a sibling who was created differently.

Friends are a source of understanding.

It's a known fact that girls process information and feelings verbally. We need to vent. We need to be heard. But most of all, we need to be understood. That's where friends come in—both guys and girls. Girlfriends can relate and empathize with us, and guy friends can offer a perspective we can't see ourselves.

Choosing the right friends takes wisdom.

When your daughter was 6 or 7, her social life was determined by her *neighborhood, school,* and *parents.* Whether she really liked little Jenny next door didn't matter much; they were automatically friends because each of them had limited options. She didn't have much say in her choice of friends and didn't know she should have a say. Oh, how things have changed!

As girls move into their teen years, friends take a position in life that is almost godlike!

key point
FRIENDS ARE KEY & CRUCIAL TO A TEEN GIRL!

With one phone call to a girlfriend, your daughter's night can be made or ruined. Her acceptance of an invitation is completely dependent on the answers of the girls in her circle. Depending on the personality and preference of your daughter, she may be sought out by many or simply looking for a few, steady, soul-sharing friends. Ultimately, she was created to be in relationship and needs healthy girls in her life to be healthy in her development. Either way, wisdom and parents need to be involved.

One of the major prayers of godly parents has to do with their teen's choice of friends. Parents who are wise understand that this choice sets a young girl on the right path or a disastrous one. With the access kids have to the Internet (chat rooms, instant messaging, blogs, and personal space pages), traveling teams, cell phones, social groups, and open enrollment, their field of choice has expanded greatly from even ten years ago. Wisdom from God is the only thing that can guide a girl through all the choices.

TARGET MOMENT

Allow your home to be grand central station for your teen's friends. Stock the fridge and the cupboards. As they mingle, you'll get a clearer picture of your teen's friends.

Guided by this wisdom, girls should look for "good" friends— ones with good hearts, solid self-esteem, and values, ones who make good choices and who have good relationships with the Lord. When a young woman aligns herself with friends who demonstrate these qualities, she has the ability to live a life free of excess pressure, self-doubt, and unhealthy conflict. Although your involvement in your daughter's choice of friends may not be received well at first, it will help shape her future relationships.

According to Chap Clark in his book *Hurt,* today's teen creates family-like bonds with friends. Because of this tight connection, influence is great, and fallouts feel like divorce to the heart of a teenager.

Parents, as much as your child would like to believe differently, you *do* need to play a guiding role in helping her choose healthy friends!

Investing in friends takes time.

Wouldn't it be great if making and maintaining friendships happened instantly? Some days I feel that would be a sweet setup, but it's not realistic. Plus, it would take away so much of the gratification in the development of friendships. Starting and maintaining true friendships certainly takes time and initiative, but girls who are willing to invest themselves will reap the rewards of lifelong friendships!

> **key point**
> **SOLID FRIENDSHIPS TAKE TIME AND EFFORT.**

> **key point**
> **WE MUST INVEST OURSELVES IN FRIENDS.**

> ✓ **MIDDLE-SCHOOL MEMOS**
>
> This is a vital time for your middle schooler! Many of the friendships she makes during this season will stay with her through high school. Watch carefully. Offer your insight and encourage the good choices you see her making.

Onions are an amazing food. If you take a close look, you'll see layer after layer of skin. Peel back one and there's another—and another, and another. Friendships have this same attribute. As girls share time and experiences, they discover new levels and characteristics of that friend and the relationship. Two girls can spend a one-hour bus ride next to each other and feel like best friends when they step off the bus!

For girls, the "peeling back process" happens much more quickly than with guys.

In his instrumental book *The Five Love Languages*, Gary Chapman describes five different ways individuals love and receive love. According to Chapman, each of us receives love in any combination of these ways.

AUTHOR GARY CHAPMAN DESCRIBES FIVE LOVE LANGUAGES:

SERVICE

QUALITY TIME

PHYSICAL TOUCH

GIFTS

WORDS OF AFFECTION

After reading *The Five Love Languages*, purchase a copy for your daughter. Encourage her to read it as a friendship enhancer. Then try to discern what the love languages are for each friend.

In a world that is so self-focused, this concept is countercultural! If girls are willing to take the time and energy to discover the love languages of their friends, the results will be amazing! For the friend who loves by words of affection, she can send a card with encouraging words. For the girl who thrives on quality time, she can be intentional about get-togethers. The end result is a blessing for all involved.

TRY THIS!

If your daughter has made a connection with another girl, invite her new friend to be part of a family weekend. During this time, you'll get a good idea of the benefits and challenges of the friendship.

Handling conflict takes guts!

key point
SOME CONFLICT IS NORMAL.

Have you ever heard someone say something like, "We never argue!" What is seen as a source of pride should really be a source of concern. A relationship that lacks conflict is an unhealthy one. Anytime two individuals with different ideas, preferences, dreams, and personalities enter into a relationship, conflict will naturally arise. The only way two people are without conflict is when one of them is holding back something and not being honest. Perhaps a common response is "Whatever" versus actually sharing an opinion, or one is stifling a part of her personality to keep conflict from coming to the surface.

Conflicts are normal and can strengthen relationships if they're handled in healthy ways.

Girls tend to shy away from conflict because of the high value they place on being connected. They imagine the worse possible outcome and often decide the pain of silence or adjustment is less than what could happen. They ignore the potential conflict and hope it goes away—which it rarely does. We need to teach our girls to face and resolve conflict in healthy, God-honoring ways instead of running away from problems.

BIG BIBLE POINT

Read Matthew 18:15-17 with your daughter and discuss why Jesus suggested conflict be handled in this way. What is God-honoring about it? Why would this be difficult?

The first step is to help your daughter check her heart through prayer. A girl must be sure she is confronting conflict for the right reasons and with a forgiven heart. Next, she should choose a non-emotional time to approach the person. If that's not possible, a handwritten note is an effective second choice. The third step is to admit she's not perfect. "I have stuff of my own that I'm working on," is a good way to start the conversation. Finally, it's important to use "I feel" statements such as, "I feel bad when you put me down in front of our friends." People can argue opinions and attacks, but they can't argue feelings!

Good friends may not always agree—but they always respect one another!

EFFECTIVE STEPS TO RESOLVING CONFLICTS

1 SEEK GOD IN PRAYER

2 APPROACH THE PERSON PERSONALLY

3 ADMIT YOU'RE NOT PERFECT

4 USE "I FEEL" STATEMENTS

Girls will spend tremendous amounts of time dodging and avoiding friends or "wanna-be friends" to save themselves the pain of confronting conflict. A teenage girl who learns to approach conflict in healthy ways will grow into a woman who handles relationships with love, forgiveness, and godliness. Why not help your daughter start on that path today?

Forgiveness first! Remind your daughter to read Ephesians 4:32 whenever conflicts arise.

Lifelong friendships bring great joy.

When girls are able to develop history within friendships, great benefits follow. The difficulty, however, is that many teenage friendships are short term. For instance, two girls can be close through middle school, but as they get older, things change. One is accepted into the "popular" crowd, and the other isn't. Or one girl is guy crazy, the other isn't, and their friendship cannot sustain the difference. Many potentially lifelong friendships are cut short because of temporary issues.

Guys and jealousy can both be the cause of short-term friendships!

✓ MIDDLE-SCHOOL MEMOS

For girls, some relationships don't make the monumental move from middle school to high school. Help your daughter know which friendships to fight for and which are better to let go.

Lifelong friends can offer a special kind of understanding that new friends simply can't.

If your daughter has a friend she's been connected with since kindergarten or even earlier, you see evidence of this understanding. They can almost speak each other's words as naturally as their own and have come to love many of the same things. When I vacationed with a new friend one year, I was longing for the understanding of my lifelong friends two days into the trip. They have what I like to call the "Heather filter." I don't need to explain myself; they just know.

key point

GIRLS LOVE SHARED EXPERIENCES!

One of the main reasons this understanding exists is because of shared experiences. Guys like to do things together, such as work on cars or play sports. But girls love to share *experiences*, to process and talk about them for the rest of their lives!

And it doesn't even have to be an official activity. Girls can make a monumental memory from doing math homework or riding the bus to a field trip. It doesn't take me long to spot girls in my junior-high ministry who have been friends since preschool. They have the most steady, loving, and deep relationships of all the girls in the ministry.

HAVE SOME FUN!

Invite a lifelong friend of yours out for a day with you and your daughter. Following the day, share with your daughter why you value this friendship.

It can strengthen relationships not to always be on the same team or be roommates at college. As close friends develop new friendships, they realize the uniqueness of their lifelong friendship, and the relationship is solidified even more.

As girls walk through their teens, college, and adulthood, events can alter friendships. Perhaps one girl moves away before eighth grade. Or friends choose different colleges. Or marriage takes one to another part of the world. As they move into different seasons, the intensity may change, but the connection remains. When those same girls reunite at a reunion or wedding, they jump back into the friendship, not skipping a beat. For girls especially, this is an essential characteristic of a relationship.

Girls love to share their lives!

Guys are a source of connection.

For many parents of teenage girls, the male population can represent fear, anxiety, and all other dreadful things. But guys can be an amazing part of your daughter's life! When a young woman develops healthy relationships with men on many levels, guys can be a source of connection and encouragement.

Relationships are a gift from God.

James 1:17 reminds us that every good gift is from God. I believe wholeheartedly this verse includes the gift of romantic relationships. As originally designed, they are meant for our pleasure and God' glory. Understanding this, we should see relationships as precious and exceptional, not commonplace and ordinary. The way we approach potential relationships should reflect this understanding.

key point
ROMANCE IS A GIFT FROM GOD.

Many teens spend more time researching the purchase of an iPod than they do researching a potential partner!

Many of you have been praying for your daughter's future husband since she was born—keep up those prayers!

What is the right time for your daughter to enter into the realm of romantic relationships? Most parents throw out the age of 16 simply from history and wanting their kids to wait. Teens, however, are confused by this rule. "What happens the night before my sixteenth birthday? Does some fairy come and sprinkle me with 'responsibility dust' or something?" They've got a good point. I know some 19-year-olds who are in no position to date—and I know a few exceptional 14-year-olds who could move toward a healthy relationship.

Does your daughter attend to chores as instructed?

Is your daughter truthful?

Does she have discernment in friends?

Is she respectful to you?

Does she have healthy self-esteem?

Has she thought through sexual purity issues and boundaries?

Instead of making a general age rule for all teens, why not determine the timing according to the individual responsibility of each person? Ask yourself questions such as these. And if the answers are positive, your "little girl" may be in a position to enter into a healthy relationship!

PARENT POINTER

The term **"going out"** in middle school simply means a guy and girl have declared themselves an item. Since they can't drive and have no real money of their own, they can't physically date, but they are excluding the possibility of another relationship forming. It's your decision as a parent to decide whether this is allowable.

When the time is right for a girl to consider a relationship, she should evaluate with caution and counsel. If her desire is to be in a God-honoring relationship, the first point of evaluation should be the condition of the heart of the boy of interest. It's not enough simply that he goes to church or, unfortunately, that he call himself a Christian. The truth lies in his behavior and his other relationships.

As much as you want to be the primary counselor for your daughter in the area of dating, it might be best for her to have the counsel of a trusted adult or family member.

DATING TIPS
FOR TEENS

✔ **BEFORE YOU SAY YES, ASK YOURSELF ...**

- Do you like the person who has asked you?
- Does this person make you feel safe?
- Do you share any interests or hobbies?
- Does this person pressure you?
- Does this person make you smile?

✔ **A BIT OF PREPARATION CAN REALLY HELP!**

SUGGEST AN ACTIVITY YOU'LL BOTH ENJOY.

The whole idea behind going out on a date is having fun. Nothing ruins this faster than choosing an activity that only one of you enjoys. Decide on something you both like, then plan your outing and time accordingly.

CONSIDER GOING OUT AS PART OF A GROUP.

If parents don't want you going out one on one, or if you feel awkward going alone, consider the safety of group dating. This is a great choice for first dates, as it lets you be more yourself by being more relaxed and secure.

BE CLEAR ON WHO'S PAYING.

If this is a first date, you may want to go "dutch" and have each of you pay for your own meals or entertainment. If you accept a date, always bring enough money to pay your own way—never assume that your date will pay for everything.

MAKE SURE YOUR PARENTS AGREE.

If your parents don't want you dating yet, respect their wishes. You may suggest a group date. Be sure your folks know where you plan on going and about what time you'll return.

DID YOU KNOW THAT ...

about 60% of teens 16-17 don't date on a regular basis?

God's gift can't be found on a clearance rack.

Ever wonder why girls are so drawn to movies like *Cinderella*? Every girl longs to be treated like a princess and be joined with a prince. The desire is not produced or manufactured,

key point

GIRLS WANT TO BE ADORED AND TREASURED.

but instilled. And as a child of the King of kings, she *is* a princess. When she sees the images in those movies, something is stirred within her. And rightly so! She deserves to be sought, protected, and adored!

key point

YOUR TEEN DAUGHTER IS A CHILD OF THE KING!

WHAT IS THE RIGHT AGE TO BEGIN DATING?

Middle-school girls begin to "search" for their prince charmings early! But when do middle-school girls believe dating should begin? Check out this chart for surprising answers!

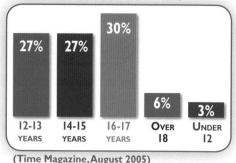

(according to 13-year-olds)

12-13 YEARS	14-15 YEARS	16-17 YEARS	OVER 18	UNDER 12
27%	27%	30%	6%	3%

(Time Magazine, August 2005)

Often, teen girls feel as if "everyone is with someone, except me." Although this conclusion is not true, it certainly feels real and can cause a girl to become anxious. Add romance-driven movies and music, and you have quite a "wanting" state of mind. At this point, a girl will be tempted to settle. Even though she longs to be treated like a princess, she'll settle for almost any guy who shows an interest in her. But settling brings nothing but second best.

TRY THIS!

Plan a girl's night for you and your daughter. Check into a hotel, have a fun supper, then watch a movie like *Ever After*. Talk about how you, as girls, long to be protected, loved, adored, and cherished.

As hard is it is to resist the temptation to settle, a girl will never regret waiting for what she deserves. I have met numerous women who would give almost anything to go back in time and erase the relationships that resulted from settling. I have never, however, heard a woman say, "I just wish I had settled more before I met my husband!" When a girl settles, she puts herself at risk for excess emotional baggage, a poor reputation, and a lifelong pattern of unhappy settling.

A girl will never regret holding out for the best!

As a discerning daughter of God, a girl needs to decide which qualities are nonnegotiable and which are negotiable.

She might think the perfect guy is tall, blonde, drives a fast car, and loves Jesus. But are all these qualities nonnegotiable? When I was younger, I wanted a guy who loved to sing karaoke because I love to sing for strangers. But in my growing wisdom with the Lord, I decided that quality was negotiable. If a girl can determine the nonnegotiable qualities she needs in a guy, those qualities will steer her away from the clearance racks.

> Help your daughter determine her "nonnegotiables" so she isn't tempted to simply *settle* for a relationship—and unhappiness!

Respect is a two-way street.

A nonnegotiable quality for all teenage girls is respect—both of oneself and of others. Imagine a device called a "respect-o-meter." Each guy your daughter is interested in should hypothetically be hooked up to the "respect-o-meter" for an assessment by the evaluation team (made up of you and your daughter). The first line of questioning would focus on respecting God as Creator, Savior, and Lord. Through the guy's actions and conversations, the team would be able to determine if he respects the one who created him.

key point

GIRLS NEED TO EXPECT RESPECT.

key point

SELF-RESPECT HONORS OUR CREATOR.

MIDDLE-SCHOOL MEMOS

The "respect-o-meter" is especially critical in the middle-school years! As your daughter shows interest in boys, help her understand how to determine if a guy is respectable or not.

Most teen guys seem to fall to the extremes—either cocky or unsure—but a healthy balance does exist, and the "respect-o-meter" can find it! Does he take good care of his body by eating right and exercising? Does he dress in a modest, respectable fashion? Does he expect to be treated with kindness and respect by your daughter? As the team observes, they'll be able to discover much about the boy's—and their daughter's—level of self-respect.

REMEMBER: Your teen models your behavior and attitudes. How is your own level of self-respect shown?

Another important area of evaluation is how a guy who likes your daughter respects his own parents (and you). A guy can talk all day about loving and respecting his parents, but putting it into action is another thing. In no way should the expectation be to find a perfect, happy, Christian home, but the genuine state of the home will communicate the tendencies and history of the young man's upbringing. If a guy has a respectful, healthy relationship with his parents, he is more likely to have healthy and respectful dating relationships. This area, like the others, takes time to evaluate, so don't make assumptions or rush to conclusions.

Read Job 38 together. Then discuss reasons why we should respect God. Also, how can a God-respecting guy be identified?

My purpose in introducing the "respect-o-meter" is not to encourage a performance-based system but to highlight the needed team effort. When a young woman enters into the dating world, she should not go alone! Sneaking out of windows and dating in secret only leads to trouble! The people who know her best and love her most should be actively involved in the process. Parents, don't envision yourself in the back seat of each date night, but *do* see yourself as part of the decision-making process.

TEEN TALK STARTERS

If you were hooked up to the "respect-o-meter," what would your scores be like?

What area of respect is most important to parents? to teens?

Do you believe that people can learn respect?

How is outward respect a sign of inward self-respect?

In what ways is having respect for self and others a way to honor God?

The pathway to purity must be traveled daily.

key point

SEX IS DISTORTED FOR OUR TEENS.

Teenagers in the twenty-first century have a perception of sex that no previous generation has had. Thanks to the Internet, movies, revealing clothing, sex-saturated music, and blatant sexual encounters on prime-time television, our kids see sex as gratification, a tool, and even power. What God intended to be one of the most incredible blessings to his children has been turned into an extracurricular activity.

key point

ABSTINENCE REQUIRES A PRIOR PLAN!

Most teenagers think their parents have no idea what it's like to be overcome with attraction concerning the opposite sex. Appropriately share some of your dating experiences with your daughter so she knows you can relate to what she is feeling.

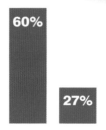

60%

27%

Only 60% of 13-year-olds in a recent study thought waiting for marriage to have sex was a good idea—the others felt it didn't really matter!

Casual intimacy is what it seemed to be for the teenage couple I confronted in the parking lot of my church. As I knocked on the steamy window of the Honda Civic, my heart was sad. The window rolled down to reveal two naked teens. After asking the strangers to leave, I walked away so disheartened. "So, this is what their picture of sex is," I thought, "Casual, rushed sex in the back of a car." How sad.

Abstinence, being willing to be set apart sexually for the Lord's glory, does not come naturally. If teens want the journey to their marriage bed to be a sexually pure one, they need to have a plan.

First, a girl needs to decide in her head and heart how far she is willing to go physically before marriage. This decision can be different for each girl and should be made *before* a physical relationship begins. Second, she needs to communicate those boundaries with the person she is dating or, better yet, hoping to date. Some teens balk at the thought of talking about sexual limits with someone they like, but if they aren't mature enough to have that kind of conversation, they certainly aren't mature enough to have an intimate relationship.

> **TARGET MOMENT**
>
> *Encourage your youth leaders to talk with the students about sex. The world is teaching your daughter —shouldn't the church present the truth of God's Word?*

> Rather than taking your daughter on a weekend getaway to discuss sex, make it a frequent, casual practice. Help her understand you're open to talking about sex without freaking out.

Next, she needs to stay out of tempting situations. If her true desire is to remain sexually pure until marriage, she needs to steer clear of being alone, horizontal, or immodestly clothed with the guy she is dating. Finally, she can't do it alone. Each teen needs to find someone to be accountable to. This person should meet the following criteria: be outside the relationship, not a parent, honest, and of the same conviction. In today's culture, a life of abstinence until marriage is a challenge, but not impossible. And our girls are worth it!

Abstinence until marriage *is* possible — even in today's society!

More Resources

BOOKS

for teens

- Mark Matlock, *Don't Buy the Lie* (Zondervan, 2004).
- Valerie Shaefer and Norm Bendell, *The Care and Keeping of You* (American Girl, 1998).
- Steven Case, *Everything Counts* (Zondervan, 2003).
- Crystal Kirgiss, *What's Up With Boys?* (Zondervan, 2004).
- Mike Yaconelli, *101 Marvelous Money-Making Ideas for Kids* (Zondervan, 1998).
- Eric and Leslie Ludy, *When God Writes Your Love Story* (Multnomah, 2004).
- J. Ortberg, *Love Beyond Reason* (Zondervan, 2001).

for parents

- Gary Chapman, *The Five Love Languages of Teenagers* (Moody Publishers, 2001).
- James Lock and Daniel le Grange, *Help Your Teenager Beat an Eating Disorder* (Guilford, 2005).
- Pam Stenzel, *Sex Has a Price Tag* (Zondervan, 2003).
- Jill Murray, *But I Love Him* (Regan Books, 2001).
- L. Parrott, *Helping Your Struggling Teenager* (Zondervan, 2000).
- Todd Cartmell, *Keep the Siblings, Lose the Rivalry* (Zondervan, 2003).

WEBSITES

- www.hearts-at-home.org (resources for stay-at-home moms and the teens they love)
- www.nationaleatingdisorders.org (information to help parents spot and deal with eating disorders)
- www.kidshealth.org/teen (real-life tips on food, fitness, and developing a healthy mind and body)
- www.helpguide.org/index.htm (expert information on emotional wellness that will last a lifetime)
- www.screenit.com/index1.html (reviews and suggestions for making wise entertainment choices)
- www.pluggedinonline.com (helpful information and insights on the world of popular entertainment)
- www.christianteens.net (Christian chat, an online youth pastor, a teen message board, and more)
- www.christianitytoday.com/teens: solid dating advice, help for living out your faith, articles about TV shows and movies, personal stories from other students, and recommendations for cool Christian music
- www.firepower.org (a site for connecting teens grades seven and up)

Subpoint Index

Chapter 1: Growing in His Image   8

Chapter 2: Godly Qualities   26

Chapter 3: Earthly Dangers 46

Chapter 4: Forming Strong Relationships 66